Philip D. Armour

111 Places
in Denver
That You Must
Not Miss

Photographs by Susie Inverso

emons:

For my mother Christina. She crossed the ocean.

© Emons Verlag GmbH
All rights reserved
© Photographs by Susie Inverso, except see p. 238
Layout: Eva Kraskes, based on a design
by Lübbeke | Naumann | Thoben
Maps: altancicek.design, www.altancicek.de
Basic cartographical information from Openstreetmap,
© OpenStreetMap-Mitwirkende, OdbL
Editing: Karen E. Seiger
Printing and binding: Grafisches Centrum Cuno, Calbe
Printed in Germany 2022
ISBN 978-3-7408-1220-1
First edition

Did you enjoy this guidebook? Would you like to see more?
Join us in uncovering new places around the world at
www.111places.com

Foreword

I've lived in the Southern Rockies since 1996. To create this book, I happily retraced my steps through Denver, allowing the city's gold to pull me this way and that. This glorious maw of streets was definitely designed for automobiles, but a generous system of bike paths snakes through parks and declares that Denver is worth slowing down for. This city is suffused by the high desert. No matter what urban, industrial, or wild place I find myself, I always feel a distinct quiet in the air, a piercing clarity to the light.

Hemmed by the Great Plains and the Rocky Mountains, the city holds its place within and against the wilderness. The fertility of the South Platte River sprouted Denver exactly, right here. I've long felt the draw, and it's energizing. My family lives in the foothills about an hour west of Downtown. One recent winter, we watched from inside the house as a mountain lion killed a deer and ate it – guts first. Moose, elk, bears, and foxes are regular visitors, too. Denver is special like this.

Denver is the region's only major city between Canada and Mexico, the economic and artistic metropolis in a vast mashup of bioregions. Small, funky mountain towns and light snow lured me here originally, but love and friendships have kept me here. Reporting this book, I was blessed by many people's generosity and vulnerability, like Mickey Mussett of Ghost Rider Boots, who laid bare his personal journey of transformation. Charleszine "Terry" Nelson, a librarian at the Blair-Caldwell African American Research Library, touched me with her story of growing up in Five Points and her community's pride and resilience.

It's prototypically Western to make something out of nothing, and Denver is a living testament to this spirit. Denver self-selects for practical yet dreamy people – people who wear flip-flops and snow boots on the same day. I'm a better person for knowing this city.

Philip D. Armour

111 Places

1 Actors' Alley

Backroom highlight of DCPA

Led Zeppelin had never played a show in the United States before they took the stage here in December 1968, opening for Vanilla Fudge. The Ellie Caulkins Opera House (then called the Denver Auditorium Arena) was the first stop of a 20-city US tour. The band did not "go down like a lead balloon," as its name suggested. Today's Denver Center for Performing Arts (DCPA) has since grown into a 12-acre site with a total of 10 theaters and is one of the largest single-site performing arts campuses in the nation. It's only rivals are Lincoln Center in Washington, DC, and the Kennedy Center in New York City.

DCPA is best known for musical theater, and Denver has been a valued stop or tour debut, for hundreds of Broadway shows – everything from *The Book of Mormon* and *Dear Evan Hansen* to *Grease* and *Little Shop of Horrors*. Actors' Alley honors every Broadway show that's ever played here, and its hallways are covered by hundreds of painted show bills, each one signed by the cast. The fractal array of hallways in the bowels of the complex are covered in this unique art-form. The general public can see the colorful tradition by signing up for tours. The giant sculpture of a blue bear on its hind legs looking into the Denver Convention Center has become an endearing symbol of Denver, but Actor's Alley is more intimate and patent.

Completed in 1908 and host of that year's Democratic National Convention, the Denver Municipal Auditorium anchors the complex. The façade is stodgy Renaissance Revival, but the 1990s remodel and expansion created a sophisticated, polished feel inside. A blown-glass chandelier by Dale Chihuly triumphantly drips from the ceiling, and a three-story mural backs the bar with famous characters from around Denver, including dance impresario Cleo Parker (see ch. 30). Step outside into the soaring, glass-topped Galleria to see the city's most unique public space.

Address 1101 13th Street, Denver, CO 80204, +1 (303) 893-4100, www.denvercenter.org | Getting there Bus 1 to Stout & 14th Streets; RTD Rail to Theater District–Convention Center (D, H Lines) | Hours See website for showtimes | Tip Access Gallery is an art gallery that showcases remarkable work made by young adults with disabilities, increasing their creative, educational, and economic opportunities (909 Santa Fe Drive, www.accessgallery.org).

2 Adams Mystery Playhouse
Kitsch with a side of quiche

Check your pretension at the door – buttoned-down Shakespearean theater this is not. However, the Bard would smile at the joyful anarchy of the live performances at Adams Mystery Playhouse. The original productions of Shakespeare's plays in the 1500s at The Globe theater in London were disorderly affairs, with hecklers and boisterous audience reactions to the action on stage and off. The playhouse follows this tradition by effectively eliminating any barriers between the stage and audience. Appropriately, its home is in a mansion that served as a mortuary for 80 years.

After serving dinner in costume and in character, the actors start the show by stepping into the audience and improvising. The ad libs are clever and spontaneous and lead to buckets of laughs. Was it a little over the top? Sure. But it's obvious every show is different, depending on the enthusiasm of that night's audience and how much everyone buys into the schtick. The occasional rimshot after eye-rolling jokes is to be expected, but this is an evening of guffaws: "You're from Chicago? Never heard of it." *Ba dum tss!*

Once the show starts, a murder quickly ensues (no matter the show), and each character's dastardly motivations are revealed. The character types are broadly portrayed and track the vaudevillian playbill: sexy *ingénue*, questionable priest, scheming doctor, unscrupulous widow, and so on. Dastardly mustaches and voluptuous bosoms abound.

The evening can be more akin to comedy club sketches than "theater," but the actors are game and the action quick. The audience is generally gleefully encouraged to drink, with singalong toasts and an intermission for resupplying at the cash bar. Each table of guests is provided with clues and called on to propel the story, including opportunities to accuse the alleged murderer before the grand *denouement*. Get ready for some raucous, ribald fun.

Address 2406 Federal Boulevard, Denver, CO 80211, +1 (303) 455-1848,
www.adamsmysteryplayhouse.com | **Getting there** Bus 31 to Federal Boulevard &
W 23rd Street | **Hours** Shows run Fri & Sat 5:45 – 8pm; see website for schedule |
Tip Room 5280 is a "live-escape game." You and your friends will have 60 minutes
to solve the clues and get out…alive (142 W 5th Avenue, www.escaperoom5280.com).

3 Adventure Forest
Aerial obstacle course for kids

Drive through downtown Denver on I-25, and you'll see this jumble of steel globes floating near the highway. Interwoven by a mishmash of rope swings, nets, slides, and ladders, the Children's Museum Adventure Forest is anchored by interconnecting steel globes and gangways that defy gravity. It's an airborne sculptural marvel – a kids' paradise, in other words, that parents can enjoy too. The Broncos may play other NFL teams across the street at Mile High stadium, but the kids have more fun here.

The metal globes are cool, shaded spaces for just hanging out. They deflect the summer heat and dangle precipitously above the neighboring rooftops and roaring highway traffic below. The perforated walls are crammed with weird ephemera to explore – little mirrors, steampunk trinkets, maps, and literary quotes. Created by artist Wes Bruce, the structure has become a Denver signature that speaks directly to the "tension between nature and city."

In addition to the physicality of traversing this structure (helmets are mandatory), the Adventure Forest invites children to decode a ciphered language along the way to interact with the Council of Creatures. They can piece together an animistic story of transformation and Earth-centered wisdom by tracking down hidden entries. It's like composing a bedtime story with your child in real time.

The kicker of the whole experience is the tunnel slide at the end. It drops precipitously into a cushioned pit and is terrifying in a kid-safe way. The rest of the Children's Museum is equally creative. The interactive, hands-on exhibits are designed to teach children about physics and natural phenomena, much like San Francisco's ground-breaking Exploratorium. Wandering the entire facility easily eats up an afternoon. And if you want more, the museum is just steps away from the fantastic Denver Aquarium. What other city aquarium has tigers?!

Address 2121 Children's Museum Drive, Denver, CO 80211, +1 (303) 433-7444, www.mychildsmuseum.org/adventure-forest | Getting there Bus 28 to W 26th Avenue & Alcott Street; RTD Rail to Union Station (A, B Lines) | Hours Wed–Sun 9am–4pm | Tip Wings Over the Rockies Air & Space Museum is for pretending you're high above the Earth. Sit in old airplanes and space equipment and make motor noises (7711 E Academy Boulevard, www.wingsmuseum.org).

4__Akihabara Arcade

Japanese otaku *culture comes to life*

Tucked away in a quiet strip mall in Westminster, this arcade is named for the Akihabara Station in downtown Tokyo, aka Electric Town. A subway stop that blossomed into a black market shopping area post World War II, the area's subversive bent has attracted and nurtured *otaku* culture over the years, which includes anime, manga, smartphones, games, and cosplay. *Otaku* loosely translates to "geek" and is a cultural identity assumed with pride.

The midday clientele at Akihabara Arcade can definitely relate. Mostly young dudes with backpacks, they sprint the cement floor to get more quarters in order not to lose their gaming progress – many games only cost 25 cents. In the side room, there's also a dedicated set of computer gamers wearing headsets and yelling into monitors. The monthly gaming tournaments livestream on Switch Media, and the competition is fierce. Ramen cups are stacked behind the bar, natch.

Owner Brandon Osha bought his first game cabinet at age 16 and never looked back. He's crafted a retro gaming haven and his collection of cabinets are all from Japan. How about taking a whirl on *Typing of the Dead* to kill zombies with a qwerty keyboard? Or loosen your hips on *Dance Revolution, Supernova 2.*

Osha's true talent, however, may be inventing sticky-sweet cocktails, like the O'Ren Ishii (watermelon liquor, vodka, and Sprite) and the Mega Man (gin, Blue Curaçao, and Sprite). His selection of Red Bull cocktails appear vaguely dangerous. Drink a supersweet Super Sonic (sour-berry vodka, lemon vodka, and blueberry Red Bull), and you may lose a tooth. And pound one – or three – Hatsune Miku (vodka, triple sec, blue curacao, and yellow Red Bull), and you're guaranteed to beat your personal record on *UFO Catcher 7.* Take note: there's a $50 service charge if you spill your drink on a game. If you prefer proper craft beer, Kokopelli Beer Company is next door.

Address 8901 Harlan Street, Westminster, CO 80031, +1 (720) 484-6610, www.akihabaraarcade.com | **Getting there** Bus 92, 100 to W 88th Avenue & Harlan Street | **Hours** Sun–Wed 6pm–midnight, Thu 2pm–midnight, Fri 2pm–2am, Sat noon–2am | **Tip** ESP HiFi is a mellow Japanese *kissaten* culture "listening café and bar" that only plays vinyl records via tube amplifiers and an impeccable sound system (1029 Santa Fe Drive, www.esphifi.com).

5__All Things Colorado

History's markers underfoot

It's ironic that these sidewalk plaques that honor Colorado are on California Street. Yes, Los Angeles may have its silly sidewalk stars devoted to famous people, but Denver has historical plaques commemorating the people and history unique to the Centennial State. Small and inconspicuously placed in the cement sidewalk on the western side of the street, these 12 square bronze plaques are about 12 inches tall. They don't scream for attention and are easy to stroll past. Just steps from the street buskers of 16th Street Mall, plaques for Jack Kerouac, Oscar Wilde, Butch Cassidy, Glenn Miller, and others round out the exclusive list of 12.

William Harrison Dempsey was born in 1895 in Manassa, a tiny farming town in Colorado's San Luis Valley. Promoted as the Manassa Mauler, this World Heavyweight Boxing Champion helped usher in the modern era of sports. Dempsey's explosive punching power and aggressive style thrilled fans and led to live radio broadcasting and huge purses. His plaque tells the comical story of becoming a boxer and earning the fighting name "Jack" Dempsey, thanks to his brother, who had his younger sibling impersonate him and fight in his stead.

A local favorite is the plaque for the eponymous Denver omelet. Also known as the Western omelet, it's made with chopped ham or bacon, onion, and bell peppers. The Denver omelet is a permanent fixture of breakfast menus nationwide, ingrained into every American's consciousness. The plaque claims the recipe was concocted "to mask the stale flavor of eggs shipped by wagon freight." Culinary historians speculate the dish was originally created by some long-lost, 19th-century "cookie" rustling grub for cowboys on cattle drives and was supposedly served on bread as a sandwich. A more-plausible theory is that Chinese railroad cooks developed the meal as transportable egg foo young.

Address California Street between 15th & 16th Streets, Denver, CO 80202 | **Getting there** RTD Rail to 16th & California Streets (D, H, L Lines) | **Hours** Unrestricted | **Tip** Build your own Denver omelet at Four Friends, the best breakfast place in town. Them's fighting words, but you've got to eat it to believe it (2893 Roslyn Street, www.fourfriendskitchen.com).

6 __ Allen Ginsberg Library
Ponder the subversiveness of originality

Poet and political activist Allen Ginsberg lived in Boulder on Bluff Street when he founded the Jack Kerouac School of Disembodied Poetics with New York poet Anne Waldman in 1974. Ginsburg was a student of Chögyam Trungpa Rinpoche (see ch. 89), who'd invited his involvement at Naropa University. Ginsberg and Kerouac had allegedly been lovers and made significant creative impact on each other. Inspired by Buddhism, drugs, sex, and music, the 1950s beatnik generation rejected the post-World War II "American Dream" and chased new and transcendent experiences instead. The resulting creative exploits arguably started the country's ongoing obsession with youth culture.

Naropa University named its library after Ginsburg in 1994 for his impact on American letters and original thought. But Kerouac was the hotter-burning beatnik. He based much of his 1957 novel *On the Road* in Denver and put the city on the pop-cultural map. Kerouac celebrated Denver's natural beauty and how it marked a crossroads at the country's geographical and spiritual heart. The United States was struggling to understand itself as desperately as he was, and Kerouac found Denver to be healing somehow.

Denver was an intersection for musicians too. Like so many other Midwesterners looking to reinvent themselves, Robert Zimmerman (born in Hibbing, Minnesota) headed west to become Bob Dylan. When he ran into the Rockies, Dylan stopped in Denver. He'd read *On the Road* by then and wanted to be washed over by the scene. He spent the summer of 1960 living in the City Park West neighborhood and playing at the Satire Lounge on E Colfax. He left under a dark cloud, though, after stealing a fellow musician's record collection.

The Allen Ginsberg Library is predictably an excellent resource for Buddhist literature. Above all, though, it's a brick-and-mortar testament to the impact of subversive creativity.

Address 2130 Arapahoe Avenue, Boulder, CO 80302, +1 (303) 2454725, www.naropa.edu/
academics/library | **Getting there** From Downtown Boulder Station, take JUMP to
Arapahoe Avenue & 21st Street | **Hours** Mon–Fri 8am–5pm | **Tip** The Denver Folklore
Center promoted Joan Baez, Arlo Guthrie, and Pete Seeger shows, establishing this acoustic
music instrument store at the center of original youth culture in Denver (1893 S Pearl Street,
www.denverfolklore.com).

7 Alliance Française

French culture celebrated daily

French-Canadian fur trappers were the first Europeans to travel the Front Range. In fact, the St. Vrain Creek, which flows through Lyons and is a major tributary of Denver's South Platte River, is named for one of them. Ceran St. Vrain partnered with William Bent to build Bent's Fort, the strategic adobe trading post in southeastern Colorado.

Alliance Française was founded in Paris in 1883 to be an international non-profit dedicated to the propagation of the French language and culture throughout France's colonial empire. Scientist and vaccine-pioneer Louis Pasteur and writer Jules Vern (*Twenty Thousand Leagues Under the Sea*) were original proponents. The organization has since grown to more than 1,000 centers worldwide in 137 countries. There are 110 centers in the US alone. Thanks to having been open since 1892, the Denver chapter is one of the largest.

The organization's venerable headquarters Maison Française, a 100-year-old brick building (571 Galapago Street) recently suffered a partial collapse. For now, operations have been moved to the International School of Denver, which hosts the bulk of the Alliance Française programs. No word yet about when the vibrant mural by Parisian artist Da Cruz that covers the building's north side will be restored. The artist's stunningly colorful and geometric style can also be seen on Cherry Creek Trail (see ch. 26).

Come here for French-language classes, and also for lectures, art exhibits, film series, wine tastings, celebrations, and cooking classes. This international organization of francophone culture is also a core member of the diverse Art District on Santa Fe Drive. It is a hub of local action. Everyone in the building speaks French, of course, and visiting French nationals find comfort here. Peruse the library, read old issues of *Paris Match* magazine, or simply enjoy an espresso at the café.

Address 206 Red Cross Way, Denver, CO 80230, +1 (303) 831-0304, www.afdenver.org, reception@afdenver.org | Getting there Bus 6, 73 to Quebec Street & 3rd Avenue | Hours Mon–Fri 9am–4pm | Tip Swedes are known for traveling to the far reaches of the world. Denver's Swedish School is the linguistic hub for this expat community of Vikings (6500 E Girard Avenue, www.svenskaskolancolorado.org).

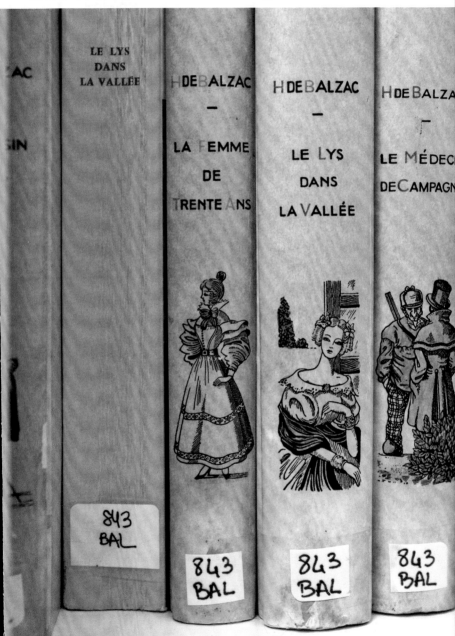

8 American Mountaineering Museum

Where the walls are for climbing

Educational and inspiring, the American Mountaineering Museum has the feel of a glossy magazine spread. There's great action photography, historical context, eccentric personalities, and the ever-present, looming threat of death. There's even a real port-a-ledge, where visitors can climb in and feel what it's like to sleep hanging from a cliff edge. Look for the crevasse exhibit spanning the museum's staircase, which shows how these glacial fissures must be navigated.

Alpinism as a sport is relatively young. It was only 1986 when Reinhold Messner became the first person to climb all 14 peaks that stand over 8,000 meters (26,246 feet), without supplemental oxygen no less. In 2019, Nirmal Purja climbed all 14 in less than seven months! It used to be that climbing at high altitude was as dangerous and remote as the idea of space travel to the moon. In the 1700s it was "scientific fact" that man-eating dragons lived high in the mountains.

Exploration seems genetically programmed into humans, and the 19th century saw an explosion of first ascents in the European Alps. Improvements in gear and clothing followed, and 20th-century explorers rarified mountaineering into a sport, pushing the difficulty of climbing routes and tackling evermore obscure firsts (speed ascents, linking summits, etc.). Summiting Mount Everest in 1953 made Sir Edmund Hillary and Tenzing Norgay worldwide celebrities. Jim Whittaker was the first American to summit Everest in 1963 – look for his actual down parka, boots, and backpack here.

The American Alpine Club has its offices and extraordinary library here, and so does the Colorado Mountain Club, which installed a massive indoor climbing wall. With nearly 700 mountains 13,000 feet and higher, Colorado has nurtured generations of mountaineers.

Address 710 10th Street, Golden, CO 80401, +1 (303) 996-2755, www.mountaineeringmuseum.org, info@mountaineeringmuseum.org | Getting there Bus 16 to 10th Street & Washington Avenue | Hours Tue – Fri 10am – 4pm, Sat noon – 5pm | Tip The founders of Übergrippen prefer to call their establishment an indoor "crag." It's still a rock climbing gym – but with a heavy focus on community and unusually long routes (8610 E 21st Avenue, www.ugclimbing.com).

9 American Museum of Western Art

Bonanza of myth-making artwork

The Navarre Building housing the American Museum of Western Art is a faithfully restored, 1880 Victorian. This period authenticity accentuates the museum's collection, which is displayed "salon style," crowding every square inch of wall space in roughly chronological order. Over 300 works burst with color and nostalgic pathos and offer a revealing immersion into Western mythmaking.

Violence and genocide conquered the American West and secured seemingly endless natural resources for settlers of European descent. The oil and gas industries created enormous wealth for some. The artistic tastes of Colorado oil billionaire Philip Anschutz are focused and accessible to today's viewers. His vision pays singular homage to the most romanticized and casually misunderstood period of American history. The landscapes and characters of the 19th-century West are cultural tropes, thanks in part to the painters who first impressed this idealism onto an eager public. The pioneering spirit inherent to the West has been celebrated and distorted ever since.

So look for *American Portrait with Flag* (1979) by Native American artist Fritz Scholder (1937–2005). It captures some of this unresolved tension within Western mythology. Abstract and defiant, the portrait is a sly confrontation of indigenous identity, experience, and painful stereotypes.

This painting's daring honesty is contrasted by the private wine cellar a level below the museum's entrance. Look down the wrought iron spiral staircase to see remnants of the subterranean service tunnel that once connected the Navarre Building to the Brown Palace Hotel (see ch. 17) under Tremont Place. Wealthy hotel patrons once used this tunnel to frequent prostitutes when the Navarre Building was a jazz club and brothel.

Address 1727 Tremont Place, Denver, CO 80202, +1 (303) 293-2000, www.anschutzcollection.org, info@anschutzcollection.org | Getting there Bus 9, 15, 20 to 17th & Welton Streets | Hours Mon, Wed, & Fri 10am–4:30pm | Tip Right next door, Homer Reed LTD has been selling tailored men's suits since 1951. The vintage shoe-shining booth, animal mounts, and gleaming wood combine for an effete atmosphere (1717 Tremont Place, www.mensclothingdenver.com).

10 Apex Gym

Zen and the art of parkour and aerial athletics

Parkour may have originated on the streets of Paris, but this kinetic art form has swept the Internet and, therefore, the world. The sport, sometimes called "freerunning," is adapted from a military training discipline and synthesizes running, climbing, and gymnastics for creative movement through space. The precise maneuvers of parkour athletes (*traceurs* for men and *traceuses* for women practitioners) can resemble those of martial artists. The leaps, flips, and spins are practiced to perfection in gyms like Apex before execution in outdoor environments, sometimes at great heights.

Instructors at Apex are almost universally former gymnasts, the type of nimble athletes typically drawn to skateboarding or trampolining. They teach good technique, safety strategies, and standard moves in a custom-built environment. This transformed warehouse is designed for three-dimensional movement, including parkour and aerial skills. Vertical, horizontal, and diagonal space is occupied by a mishmash of monkey bars, boxes, I-beams, and pads. Athletes run, jump, vault, and tumble across the obstacles with balletic grace and power.

Today's parkour gyms are what trampoline gyms were 10 years ago: fresh and breathtakingly original. Who'd ever heard of a "progression environment" before parkour hit the scene in the early aughts? The use of obstacle courses for training is nothing new in law enforcement, firefighting, and the military, but their transformation into creative spaces for play is weirdly intuitive. To anyone who's ever scaled a fence for style points, jumped from a tree, or rolled on the lawn, Apex will feel like a homecoming to childhood – with grip tape and springy floors.

The first Apex opened in Boulder in 2006, and today there are three gyms across the Front Range offering varied course selection for all ages and skill levels. Parkour and aerial training are fun alternatives to your all-too-familiar workouts.

Address 700 W Mississippi Avenue, Building A, Apt. 5, Denver, CO 80223, +1 (720) 454-2857, www.apexdenver.com, apexmovementdenver@gmail.com | Getting there Bus 11, 14 to W Mississippi Avenue & S Galapago Street | **Hours** Mon–Fri 4–10pm, Sat 10am–5pm, Sun 11am–5pm | **Tip** Try the "Ninja Warrior" course at SkyZone Trampoline Park. Safe and outrageously shaped, the obstacles and trampolines at this facility are a kid's dream. Be as rough as you want – upside down (7330 W 52nd Street, Arvada, www.skyzone.com/arvada).

11 Apothecary Farms
Experts in extracted cannabis oils

Purchasing marijuana in Denver can be overwhelming. There are more than 570 recreational dispensaries and nearly as many methods of consumption. Just down the street from Habibi Hookah Café, Wake & Bake donut shop, and several competing dispensaries, Apothecary Farms narrows the confusing options. This dispensary focuses almost exclusively on extracted oils, concentrates, and "pure, live resin." When this Denver location opened in 2019, it sold zero "flower" (aka marijuana buds). The product line has since expanded, but the devotion to concentrates makes Apothecary Farms special.

Think of extracted products as turbo-boosted marijuana – all the cannabinoid-rich oil without the combustible plant matter. Concentrates are typically heated into vapor, not burned. None of the products sold here are diluted with other oils for viscosity (also unique among competitors), and the vape pens are free of solvents, glycerin, or MCT oil. Apothecary Farms preserves terpenes and cannabinoids throughout the extraction process, which maximizes fragrance and strength.

"Dabbing" these products (inhaling vaporized concentrates) releases massive amounts of THC and is not for newbies. Vape pens, however, are easy to dose by puffing one toke at a time. Apothecary Farms does sell pre-rolled joints, edibles, and some flower grown by close partners, but only the company-grown flower is used for making the concentrates. Apothecary Farms is also "vertically integrated," owning their own growing operation, extraction/production facility, and dispensary. This structure allows for quality control throughout the process and competitive pricing.

Colorado pioneered smart, safe recreational marijuana sales in 2008, and civic society has not imploded. Be aware, however, that it's easy to consume too much. The mindful budtenders at Apothecary Farms will steer you right.

Address 2251 S Broadway, Denver, CO 80210, +1 (303) 862-5016, www.apothecaryfarms.com | Getting there Bus 0 to Broadway & W Iliff Avenue | Hours Daily 8am–9:50pm | Tip BYOC (Bring Your Own Cannabis) to the Coffee Joint (1130 Yuma Court, www.thecoffeejointco.com) or Tetra Private Lounge & Garden (3039 Walnut Street, www.tetralounge.com) for open consumption of cannabis on site.

12 Ashtanga Yoga Denver
Traditional instruction for union

Serious yogi or just yoga curious? Go to The Cube. The big spaces here accommodate the expressiveness of yoga. All skylights and soaring ceilings, this square building is a former art gallery that now hosts Ashtanga Yoga Denver. To enter the practice room, students step across beautifully carved wooden thresholds, tactile talismans sourced in southern India to remind all that yoga's intentional movement and breathing are deliberate formulas for change.

The Sanskrit language and utterly foreign trappings of yoga can be off-putting to Westerners wanting to relax or just shrink their midsections, but there is benefit from seeking more classical instruction. The teachers at Ashtanga Yoga Denver are seriously versed in the traditional tenets of *hatha* (physical) yoga, which means students receive foundational instruction that they can develop further on their own or at less-rigorous yoga studios.

Ashtanga (eight-limbed) yoga was developed by K. Pattabhi Jois and taught for decades at his yoga *shala* in Mysore, India. He is the modern originator of a set of hatha yoga poses (*asana*) and breathing techniques (*pranayama*) that connect into a flow of consecutive movements (*vinyasa*) – since rebranded "power yoga" or "yoga flow" in the West. This forceful style of hatha yoga is particularly effective for athletes looking to improve balance, stamina, and core strength.

Meanwhile, the phrase "mindfulness" has devolved into a synonym for "woke." When approached with healing intent, any activity can be a spiritual practice, of course, and Ashtanga Yoga can be downright transformative – without the self-righteousness. The rhythmic, highly physical movements and connected breathing helps one surrender to the *asana* and allow the poses to rework your body, inside and out. The discipline required to learn the sequential moves of the primary series of *asana* sharpens the mind, too.

Address 2501 Larimer Street, Denver, CO 80205, www.denverashtangayoga.com | Getting there Bus 44 to Larimer & 25th Streets; RTD Rail to Welton & 27th Streets (L Line) | Hours See website for class schedule | Tip Across the street, BIG Power Yoga offers more of a yoga-as-lifestyle class and social format (2470 Broadway, www.bigpoweryoga.com).

13 Babi Yar Memorial Park

Renewal by remembrance

Walking through this park is a somber meditation on resilience in the face of cruelty. The natural splendor and elegant design make an obvious impact, but the park's intent and educational history strike the heart. Memorials like this are essential to keeping history alive and informing more ethical behavior in the body politic. Babi Yar Memorial Park is a protest and a celebration – beauty will endure, no matter what.

From 1941–1943, the Axis powers (mostly German soldiers) murdered approximately 100,000 people in Kyiv, Ukraine and dumped them in a ravine. The Babi Yar ravine outside Kiev still serves as a mass grave for Jews, Roma, communists, Soviet prisoners of war, Ukrainian nationalists, and others. The genocide of Jews in World War II was emblematic of a German state determined to control not just bloodlines but history itself. The Nazis used murder and terror to eliminate dissent of any kind. Babi Yar Memorial Park challenges this tragic failure by artfully holding individual dignity above ideology.

Run in association by the Mizel Museum and Denver Parks & Recreation, this 27-acre park looks inconspicuous from the road. But this modesty is shattered by the hard truths of Babi Yar chiseled into severe, black granite. You enter through a narrow passage between monoliths of stone, an airy doorway that seems to indicate fragility amid stolid circumstances. Walk the park's centralized pathway, which is configured as a Star of David, and stop at the three main architectural features: an amphitheater, a grove, and a ravine.

The ravine is crossed by a bridge of tall black wood, meant to resemble the cattle cars that delivered Holocaust victims. The Grove of Remembrance is planted with 100 linden trees to represent the dead and arranged in a geometric pattern. The People's Place amphitheater focuses on the landscape, with berms and an elevated platform. Be transformed.

Address 10451 E Yale Avenue, Denver, CO 80231, +1 (720) 785-7300, www.mizelmuseum.org, dctails@mizelmuseum.org | Getting there Bus 83D, 105 to S Havana Street & Yale Avenue | Hours Daily dawn–dusk | Tip Mizel Museum is Denver's cornerstone of Holocaust education, Jewish culture, and social justice (400 S Kearney Street, www.mizelmuseum.org).

14 Billy's and Biker Jim's
Haute dogs for the people

The concept of a "gourmet hot dog" sums up the Denver zeitgeist: working class chic. Biker Jim's Gourmet Hot Dogs and Billy's Gourmet Hot Dogs are two businesses in town that incorporate the phrase. Billy's prides itself on all-beef hot dogs served with a dizzying array of condiments, while Biker Jim's specializes in game meat. Owned by a Harley-Davidson-loving biker, Biker Jim's serves hotdogs in every shape, flavor, and size made from rattlesnake, ostrich, reindeer, wild boar, elk, and more. Try the "mythically delicious" jackalope dog that's infused with cherry and habanero. Another local favorite, Mustard's Last Stand in Boulder definitely wins for best name, but their hot dogs, while tasty, are "normal" in comparison.

Biker Jim's restaurant feels industrial, like it could be a garage for fixing motorcycles – all brick, steel, and concrete. Owner Jim Pettinger is a former repo man, and there's a wall-sized photo of him reclining on his Harley-Davidson, with his feet up on the handlebars. The company logo is a stylized skull that looks like a graffiti tag, which Jim also has tattooed on his back. He started with pushcart on the 16th Street Mall and has the kind of boisterous personality that attracted Anthony Bourdain to feature him in a *No Reservations* episode about the Denver food scene.

Both restaurants pull people in off the street with the familiar aromas of backyard grilling. And both are on Larimer Street, short walks from Coors Field. Biker Jim's has a booth inside Coors Field, and Billy's has a booth inside Ball Arena. To accommodate the crowds that spill from Larimer Street's densely packed bars, Biker Jim's stays open till 3:00am and Billy's till midnight. Larimer's colorful street life is accentuated by cool historic touches, like the ancient mural painted on a building at the corner of 21st Street. It advertises Lipton Tea and Strongfortism, a workout regimen from the 1930s that "builds muscular men."

Address Biker Jim's, 2148 Larimer Street, Denver, CO 80205, +1 (720) 746-9355, www.bikerjimsdogs.com; Billy's, 2445 Larimer Street, Denver, CO 80205, +1 (303) 284-2714, www.billysgourmethotdogs.com | Getting there Biker Jim's: Bus 8, 38 to Larimer & 22nd Streets; Billy's: Bus 48 to Broadway & Walnut Street | Hours See websites | Tip Edwards Meats has an excellent selection of wild game for grilling at home (12280 W 44th Avenue, Wheat Ridge, www.edwards-meats.com).

15 _ Blair-Caldwell Research Library

Setting the record straight

The African American Spirit of the West bas-reliefs on the front of the Blair-Caldwell African American Research Library were created by Denver artist Thomas Jay Warren. Massive and stark, they depict African American faces in profile against backgrounds of mosaic tile. The subjects appear frozen in determined stares, powerful in their simplicity. Perhaps they are confronting the path ahead – hard truths are kept, documented, and studied inside this library. There is no place for political persuasion or apathy when acknowledging the daily reality of institutional racism.

One of 26 branches of the Denver Public Library system, the Blair-Caldwell African American Research Library is a guiding star of the Five Points neighborhood. The 40,000-square-foot building opened in 2003 after years of persistent lobbying for an educational institution that accurately reflected the experience of African Americans in Denver. It celebrates the community in photos and original documents, establishing the veracity that Black people helped shape Colorado and the modern West.

A wing of the second floor celebrates the achievements of Denver's prominent African Americans, including Tuskegee Airmen, the primarily Black military bomber and fighter pilots and airmen of World War II. These fighters, like many Jim Crow-era African Americans, were forced to overachieve to reach "equality." They fought with deadly efficiency, despite being excluded from training and from serving with white servicemen and, in some cases, despite being provided with outdated airplanes and equipment. The stories of suppression and success presented in the large third-floor educational exhibit are also impactful.

The library also borders historic Sonny Lawson Park, the once vibrant baseball park where Negro League teams competed.

Address 2401 Welton Street, Denver, CO 80205, +1 (720) 865-2401,
history.denverlibrary.org/blair | **Getting there** Bus 43 to California & 25th Streets; RTD
Rail to 27th & Welton Streets (L Line) | **Hours** Tue–Fri 10am–6pm, Sat 10am–5pm | **Tip**
The Black American West Museum & Heritage Center is located in the former home of
Dr. Justina Ford, the first licensed, female, African American doctor in Denver. The displays
tell the stories of Black cowboys, miners, soldiers, homesteaders, ranchers, blacksmiths,
schoolteachers, and lawmen of the West (3091 California Street, www.bawmhc.org).

16 Bound by Design
Tattoo you and your tribe

Is there a form of physical self-expression that's more universal in today's America than a tattoo? People's attraction to body ink spans the political spectrum, generations, and genders. Approximately 30 percent of Americans have at least one tattoo, with 50 percent of those people getting tattooed within the last decade – statistics that skew younger and are inextricably linked to the rise of social media.

People crave a sense of belonging, and the tribe of the tattooed is naturally inclusive. It's a common language that Denverites have embraced enthusiastically. Bound by Design, in the neon-bright Colfax Avenue strip of Capitol Hill, has a crew of extremely talented artists fluent in a variety of modern and more-classic tattoo styles. The types of tattoo styles and subject matter vary dramatically, which is part of the culture's appeal. Selecting and bonding with your Bound by Design artist will form all-important trust. Getting a tattoo is a vulnerable process – there's blood and pain. The shop also offers body piercings, the attendant fetish of tattoo culture.

Opened in 1993, Bound by Design has a mellow yet professional vibe, which makes it good for people looking to get inked for the first time. (Sworn Oath in Arvada is also known for being very accommodating for first-timers.) Don't want to go all the way? Try a temporary henna design. This plant-based ink rubs off in a few weeks.

The profusion of tattoo parlors in Denver is astonishing. Like breweries and marijuana dispensaries, tattoo shops are ubiquitous here. Business is booming, and the most successful artists have strong social media followings. The Bound by Design staff is trained to instill confidence and calm, and the studio is a clean, safe environment. You'll never be the same after a tattoo, and that's the point – self-transformation in the spirit of joining a tribe of the initiated.

Address 1332 E Colfax Avenue, Denver, CO 80218, +1 (303) 832-8282, www.boundbydesign.com | **Getting there** Bus 15 to Colfax Avenue & Downing Street | **Hours** Daily 11am–9pm (closed 3:30–4:30pm) | **Tip** Head for the Denver Selfie Museum to show the social media world your freshly ink-augmented self (1531 Stout Street, www.denverselfiemuseum.com).

17__Brown Palace Hotel
Presidential and plebeian room and board

Thankfully, some things never change. The Grande Dame of Denver hotels and its mighty, rough-hewn red granite and sandstone façade are here to stay. The building's odd, triangle shape even defines the course of several downtown streets. And since 2010, the hotel has been at the forefront of urban beekeeping! Five hives are kept on the roof, with surplus honey being used to make annual batches of everything from mead and infused bourbon to lip balm and soap.

No one knows if mead was on the menu in 1911, but that's when a jealous suitor vying for a wealthy (already married) socialite shot and killed his competitor and an innocent bystander in the hotel bar. But this bloodshed has not stopped every sitting US president but four from staying at the Brown Palace. Dwight D. Eisenhower even dubbed it, "The Western White House," after using the hotel during his presidential campaign. Even the Beatles stayed here when they played Red Rocks in 1964.

The $2 million it cost to build "The Brown" in 1892 equals $56 million in today's dollar. It was Denver's tallest building and one of the first fireproof buildings in the country. Older than the Colorado State Capitol (see ch. 65), it draws water from its own artisanal well, 720 feet deep. The Brown also has underground tunnels that lead to nearby buildings, including a former brothel (see ch. 9).

Like the rest of Denver, the hotel embraces the National Western Stock Show come January. The year's Grand Champion Steer is penned in the magnificent grand atrium for a few weeks before being shipped off to slaughter. But visit any time of year for the Victorian tradition of Afternoon Tea, served daily since the hotel's opening. Stuff your face with finger sandwiches, scones, and desserts, and drink tea with Devonshire cream. And, of course, sweeten your cup with honey harvested from the rooftop beehives.

Address 321 17th Street, Denver, CO 90202, +1 (303) 297-3111, www.brownpalace.com | **Getting there** Bus 20 to 17th Avenue & Broadway | **Hours** See website for dining options | **Tip** On a smaller scale, the Boulderado Hotel, is just as old and charming as the Brown. It also draws from an artisanal well, and the stained glass that tops the central atrium was imported from Italy (2115 13th Street, Boulder, www.boulderado.com).

18 Buckhorn Exchange

Rocky Mountain oysters served fresh

When you do land office business in balls, no one is going to demolish your building. The Buckhorn Exchange was awarded Denver's very first liquor license after Prohibition and has been selling whiskey and Rocky Mountain oysters for 130 years. A 19th-century brick behemoth, it's a lonely sentinel among rows and rows of gleaming apartment buildings. The long, narrow, windowless walls are a testament to the neighboring buildings, now flattened. It once served thirsty railroad workers and is essentially the rustic prototype for every cowboy steakhouse in the country, wagon-wheel fence and all.

Also nicknamed "cowboy caviar," "prairie oysters," "calf fries," and "Montana tendergroins," bull testicles are deep-fried and chewy. The slices are reminiscent of bland calamari. You might say bovine castration is more veterinary practice than gastronomic delight. So just smile and heap on the horseradish and cocktail sauce. A certain pride is won for having crossed this Rubicon.

The Buckhorn Exchange feels immortal. The walls swerve and the floorboards creak, but the building's age is locked in time. The original bar, a stubborn relic from 1857, was carved in Germany from white oak. It was transported to Denver via ship, rail, and covered wagon. Remarkably, two of the glass panes reflecting the top-shelf liquor are original.

The restaurant's first owner was personal friends with Teddy Roosevelt, Buffalo Bill Cody (see ch. 20), and Sitting Bull. He was an avid hunter, and 550 animal trophies crowd the walls. There's an exceptionally rare white buffalo, sacred to certain Native American tribes. The standing Kodiak brown bear seems poised for selfies. There are 250 historic firearms on display, and every corner hides an artifact, like John F. Kennedy's 1960 Colorado fishing license. He used the Buckhorn Exchange as headquarters when campaigning in Denver for the presidency.

Address 1000 Osage Street, Denver, CO 80204, +1 (303) 534-9505, www.buckhorn.com |
Getting there RTD Rail to 10th Avenue & Osage Street (D, E, H Lines) | Hours
Mon–Thu 5–9pm, Fri–Sun 4:30–9:30pm | Tip The Fort is an adobe-style complex
hemmed by sandstone cliffs in Morrison. The restaurant's fur-trapper décor suits the wide
selection of game meat, including Rocky Mountain oysters (19192 CO-8, Morrison,
www.thefort.com).

19 __ Buell Public Media Center
Wellspring of public broadcasting

Can a culture be great without great art? In a word, no. Take a tour of
the Buell Public Media Center to feel this authenticity. The building
houses an all-star cast of broadcasters, including jazz radio station
KUVO (89.3 FM). This bedrock cultural institution is one of a few
local radio stations that airs Black DJs daily. It broadcasts a charac-
teristically broad spectrum of music, from jazz and fusion to salsa and
blues. The signature Latin Soul Party (Fridays 8 p.m.) is regularly
voted Denver's favorite radio show.

Walk through the 93,000 square-foot building, and peek into the
Phyllis A. Greer Performance Studio to see musicians of all types
perform live broadcasts. Rocky Mountain PBS anchors the Buell
Public Media Center, which also houses a community media center
for students, Masterpiece performance studio, COLab newsroom,
and more. The building is a hive of community-centric activity and
a direct extension of historic Five Points.

Five Points, once known as Harlem of the West, is on the northeast side of downtown and was named for the intersection of five city
streets. It marks the end of the downtown grid and the start of more
residential neighborhoods that ring the city's heart. Discriminatory
home-sale policies and segregation limited housing opportunities in
Denver from the post-Civil War era into the early 20th century, so
African Americans made Five Points their own. They filled it with
Black-owned businesses and institutions, and today the neighborhood is a Historic Cultural District.

At its best, Buell Public Media Center is a publicly funded
loudspeaker for "the values and cultural diversity" of Denver. A
$6 million-donation from the Buell Foundation made it possible.
Colorado architect Temple Hoyne Buell, the foundation's founder,
designed the Paramount Theater and the Cherry Creek Shopping
Center (see ch. 26).

Address 2101 Arapahoe Street, Denver, CO 80205, +1 (303) 480-9272, www.rmpbs.org/ buellpublicmediacenter | Getting there Bus 44, 48 to Broadway & Arapahoe Street | Hours See website to book tours | Tip Opened in 1931, Denver Fire Station No. 3, aka Pride of the Points, is Denver's oldest and smallest active fire station and was exclusively manned by Black firefighters until the department was desegregated in 1958. It's said to be haunted after a series of tragedies (2500 Washington Street, www.denverfireonline.com).

20__Buffalo Bill's Grave

Wild West Show ringmaster rests in peace, mostly

William F. "Buffalo Bill" Cody was America's first entertainment superstar. He promoted himself relentlessly and became "famous for being famous," setting the mold for modern celebrity. His *Wild West Show* was an entertainment spectacle on a scale no one had ever seen. The rollicking performances captured people's fantasies of the West, with dangerous heroes and sympathetic villains. Cody's cast of animals, vehicles, and equipment was so massive, the US Army actually studied his methods for efficient loading and unloading of the freight from train cars.

He toured the globe with *Buffalo Bill's Wild West Show*, expertly selling the American myth to millions, including the Queen of England. The settling of the West was a violent clash of indigenous cultures and modern land lust, and Cody was Zelig-like in his associations. An alleged buffalo hunter, Pony Express rider, Army scout, and Indian fighter, Cody was present as Europeans plowed west to realize Manifest Destiny. His life spanned – and came to symbolize – an era of unprecedented change.

Cody went on to found the town of Cody, Wyoming, where the hotel he built and named after his daughter Irma operates to this day. When Buffalo Bill died in Denver in 1917, he lay embalmed for six months until a proper road could be constructed to his requested burial spot on Lookout Mountain. But Wyoming residents wanted him buried in the Cowboy State, and a rumor circulated that Cody's body had been stolen from the mortuary and replaced with a vagrant. Cody's grave here is ringed by black wrought iron and covered in tons of concrete to deter theft.

The adjacent Buffalo Bill Museum is packed with clothes and gear that belonged to the famous ringmaster. The peace pipe owned by Sitting Bull is particularly moving. The playbills and dime novels are full of hyperbole, on which Cody gladly capitalized.

Address 987 1/2 Lookout Mountain Road, Golden, CO 80401, +1 (720) 865-2160, www.buffalobill.org | **Getting there** By car, take I-70 west to Exit 256. Turn right at the top of the ramp, and then an immediate left. Turn right on Lookout Mountain Road. | **Hours** See website for seasonal hours | **Tip** The Mines Museum of Earth Science houses actual moon rocks, plus the Colorado minerals and fossils that define the state (1310 Maple Street, Golden, www.mines.edu/museumofearthscience).

21 Buffalo Herd Overlook
Roam on the range

The only city-maintained bison herd in the country grazes the foothills of Golden, Colorado. Approximately two dozen animals plod 2,413-acre Genesee Park. You may see them from your car just off I-70 at Exit 254.

When explorer and cartographer John C. Frémont (1813–1890) traveled through this area, an estimated 30–60 million bison roamed North America. He led five expeditions throughout the West between 1842 and 1853 to map the state and survey railroads – Denver's Fremont Street is named after him.

Bison were the backbone of many Native American cultures and remain vital today. Once numbering almost 60 million, only about 1,000 bison survived by the turn of the 19th century. The wholesale slaughter of bison was driven by colonial greed and violent genocide, and by an explicit policy by the US Government to starve and conquer native peoples during the so-called Indian Wars west of the Mississippi (1811–1924).

This herd's bison were transplanted from Yellowstone about 100 years ago and retain the wild traits that made them intrinsic to the prairie. They can jump six feet in the air, even at 2,000 pounds, and outrun horses. Their thick coats help withstand brutal winter blizzards, and they rotate on their front legs (not rear, like a horse), allowing them to pivot and face or kick wolves with blinding speed. You can feel their power even from across the fences.

Look west from Buffalo Herd Nature Preserve to behold the Continental Divide, the snow-covered chain of summits that defines the east and west watersheds of the Rocky Mountains. Southwest, above Georgetown, rests 14,065-foot Mount Bierstadt, named for German-American painter Alfred Bierstadt (1830–1902), who painted sumptuous oil paintings of bison and helped popularize their preservation. He also rendered dramatic landscapes of Estes Park.

Address Exit 254, I-70, Golden, CO 80401, www.uncovercolorado.com/wildlife/buffalo-herd-nature-preserve | Getting there Drive I-70 W to Exit 254 | Hours Unrestricted | Tip Visit Orr's Trading Company to pick up a buffalo skull for the mantle. Orr's also sells Native American arts and craft materials for making ceremonial dance regalia (3422 S Broadway, Englewood, www.orrs.com).

22   Buyer Beware Plaque
Ode to an infamous con man

At the corner of 17th and Larimer Streets, you'll find a bronze sidewalk plaque that reads, *Let the Buyer Beware*. It's a historic tribute to swindler Jefferson Randolph "Soapy" Smith.

Smith (1860–1898) ran gambling and prostitution rings near here in the late 1800s, though earning his nickname as a traveling salesman. Smith would roll into town after town and bark to draw a crowd, claiming his $5 bars of soap had $100 bills tucked into a select few. When a plant would shout for joy after "discovering" $100 in his wrapper, soap sales would be brisk…briefly.

Originally from Georgia, Smith worked as a cowboy in Texas, but hard labor had soured him. He moved to Colorado and launched a series of cons instead. One of his ploys was the discovery of a prehistoric, petrified, 10-foot-tall man, a statue he'd buried in Creede. Smith charged the local silver miners to see his fraudulent figure – then skipped town, as usual.

In Denver, gambling, prostitution, and sleight-of-hand shell games and card games were lucrative enough that Smith bribed local politicians and police for protection. He was also known for generosity, donating to churches and civic organizations. A sign above the door at one of his establishments allegedly read in Latin, "Caveat Emptor," or "Let the buyer beware." When the new Governor of Colorado fired three corrupt officials in 1894, they refused to vacate their offices in Denver City Hall. The state militia was called to break up the standoff, prompting Smith, who had prior been commissioned deputy sheriff, and his cronies to climb to the top of Denver City Hall with rifles and dynamite to exonerate their friends. It's a miracle no one was killed. This crazy event is remembered as the City Hall War.

Smith then moved to Skagway, Alaska, to exploit his anonymity and fleece miners in the Klondike Gold Rush. He was killed there in a shootout at just 37 years old.

Address Southwest corner of 17th & Larimer Streets, Denver, CO 80202 | Getting there Bus 0, 1, 6 to 17th & Lawrence Streets | Hours Unrestricted | Tip Soapy Smith Brewing Company pays homage to Colorado's infamous charlatan with a selection of distinctly truthful beers. Try the excellent Swindler hazy IPA (1713 14th Street, www.soapysmithbrewing.weebly.com).

23 Casa Bonita Rebooted

American-style Mexican fiestas nightly

It's official: Life does, in fact, imitate art. The creators of *South Park* Trey Parker and Matt Stone proved the old saw by purchasing Casa Bonita for $3.1 million in 2021, thereby snatching the Lakewood restaurant from the jaws of bankruptcy. Seating up to 1,000 diners at a time, this 52,000-square-foot "Mexican village" embodies a unique kind of mayhem. *South Park*'s Cartman resorted to kidnapping and worse in season 7, episode 11 to taste the intoxicating nectar of this place. The mix of mariachis, puppet shows, and haunted pirate tunnels proves both overwhelming and irresistible in real life. And nothing says "fine dining" like a phallic pink clocktower and multi-tiered water fountain in a strip mall parking lot.

Hopefully, Casa Bonita will remain a family restaurant at its core. Parker and Stone plan to remodel but, more importantly, they plan to upgrade the menu. But some things simply cannot be improved upon. Children are meant to run amok between fake palm trees, and servers are meant to scrape up spilled milk shakes from carpets with brooms and dustpans. It won't be long before Indeed.com runs posts for actors to don the notorious gorilla suit.

Casa Bonita has been in continuous operation since 1974, hosting generations of Colorado birthday parties. The original Casa Bonita was in Oklahoma City, Oklahoma, with similar "eatertainment" restaurants under the same brand in Tulsa and Little Rock, Arkansas, all since closed. This "Disneyland of Mexican restaurants" may be a caricature of itself, but hand-standing cliff divers that launch flips off a 30-foot platform are worth fighting for.

The advocacy group Save Casa Bonita certainly thinks so. They've been holding fundraisers and selling merchandise to raise money for the cause because it's not dinner without cowboy gunfight reenactments over an indoor waterfall. Yes, Casa Bonita serves tequila. You're going to need it.

Address 6715 W Colfax Avenue, Lakewood, CO 80214, +1 (303) 232-5115, www.casabonitadenver.com | Getting there Bus 16 to W Colfax Avenue & Pierce Street | Hours Sun–Thu 11am–9pm, Fri & Sat 11am–10pm | Tip Los Carboncitos is the kind of Mexican restaurant where Mexicans actually eat (several locations, www.loscarboncitoscolorado.com). *Muy sabroso!*

24__Cervantes' Masterpiece
Ballrooms for dancing all night long

Music aficionados immediately mention the Paramount, Dazzle, or the Bluebird Theater as the places to see national acts when they play Denver. Fair enough. But the Cervantes' Masterpiece Ballroom goes harder. This is the locals' local joint for live music of every genre, not just jazz.

Yes, the Levitt Pavilion hosts free outdoor concerts, and you can see good Colorado-bred talent at Larimer Lounge, but Cervantes' is set up for dancing to live musicians late into the night (er, morning) in two cavernous ballrooms – The Other Side (500 people) and Cervantes' Ballroom (900 people) – with acres of hardwood and a steady stream of incredible acts. Need a breather? The outdoor smoking area is a peaceful oasis with seating.

Originally called the Casino Cabaret, this old building dates back to the 1930s. Duke Ellington, Count Basie, and Benny Goodman took the stage here, later followed by B.B. King, James Brown, Ray Charles, and Ike & Tina Turner. Nothing can ever replicate the legendary grittiness of the former Café Chapultepec, but Cervantes' has absorbed the authenticity of a parade of groundbreaking acts. The massive wall art celebrating Miles Davis, Dizzy Gillespie, and Louis Armstrong hints to everything that's gone down here.

People come here to dance. The sound systems are acoustically perfect, technical masterpieces that envelop you completely. Whether it's the heavy metal Summer Slaughter Tour or a horn-heavy ensemble that plays hypnotic jams by Fela Kuti, the music rips, and the crowd responds enthusiastically. Pass The Peas is an eatery in The Other Side that serves fresh healthy sandwiches and more, focusing on locally sourced and organic ingredients. Stepping out into the night after a sweaty boogie can be a reality check, though. There's an active homeless community in this neighborhood, and the late-night streets teem with activity.

Address 2637 Welton Street, Denver, CO 80205, +1 (303) 297-1772, www.cervantesmasterpiece.com | **Getting there** Bus 43 to California & 27th Streets | **Hours** Daily 7pm–2am | **Tip** The Ogden Theater was built in 1919 and retains a touch of grandeur. Harry Houdini performed here! Today, it's a perennial hotspot for live music (935 E Colfax Avenue, www.ogdentheatre.com).

25_ Chamberlin Observatory
Reach for the skies

The Chamberlin Observatory has been serving astrophiles and space cadets since the 19th century. It's remarkable to think the space-curious have been studying here since the era of steam trains and horse-drawn carriages. The sandstone building, completed in 1894, looks modern somehow, gracefully matching form to function. The red stone was quarried from Lyons yet looks like it sprang to life in place, tucked into a copse of trees. The building, which is on the National Register of Historic Places, has a silver-colored dome of galvanized iron that proclaims scientific inquiry is practiced here.

The observatory anchors the eponymous Observatory Park in the University Park neighborhood. University of Denver owns and operates the building, but the public is allowed access via outreach programs hosted by the university. The members-only Denver Astronomical Society, the local champions of "astronomical history, lore, and phenomena," also studies here.

The 26-foot-long telescope assembly is precisely balanced on a 4.5-ton cast-iron pillar that's supported atop a 25-foot-tall, 320-ton pillar of red sandstone blocks extending into the reinforced basement. All this mass ensures that zero vibration disturbs viewing. The observatory's 20-inch refracting doublet lens is legitimately large even by today's standards and is perfectly balanced. The telescope swivels with a light touch of the hand.

Denver is one mile closer to the stars than most places, but the city's exponential increase in light pollution over the last 120 years has reduced contrast. It's more difficult today to see astronomical objects, especially faint ones, like nebulae or galaxies. To escape city lights, the Denver Astronomical Society built the Edmund G. Kline Dark Sky Site on the remote plains near Deer Trail (see ch. 39). Dark Sky Weekends are held there monthly near the new moon for optimal viewing.

Address 2930 E Warren Avenue, Denver, CO 80210, +1 (303) 756-1421, www.science.du.edu/physics/chamberlin-observatory, info@denverastro.com | Getting there Bus 21 to Evans Avenue & S Milwaukee Street | Hours Tue & Thu 8:30pm (summer), 7:30pm (winter) | Tip The Fiske Planetarium at University of Colorado in Boulder offers a wide range of astronomy- and physics-related programs (2414 Regent Drive, Boulder, www.colorado.edu/fiske).

26 Cherry Creek Park

Cherry pick activities in this shopping haven

Cherry Creek Park and Cherry Creek Trail are sterling examples of good urban planning. This trail is a fast and efficient route for bicycle travel through the city, and it bisects parks with blooming trees and flowers. Denver's cherry trees in springtime are a signature event. Link up with the High Line Canal Trail, too, and see the city's neighborhoods from car-free angles.

Not to be confused with Cherry Creek State Park in Aurora (also worth visiting for the lake and camping), Cherry Creek Park skirts Cherry Creek Shopping Center, Denver's high-end shopping mall and the surrounding pedestrian-friendly shopping district. This area did, in fact, have commercial cherry growing 100 years ago, with more than 500,000 trees in production in Northern Colorado, though it was named for the chokecherry bushes that lined the riverbanks. The small pockets of cherry trees that remain today pay homage to the canned cherries that once shipped around the country. The shortages of World War II and a series of freezes effectively shut down the industry.

Visit Cherry Creek Shopping Center for Hermès and Tiffany, but wander the neighborhood for little gems like Revampt, a retail boutique specializing in home decor made from handcrafted from repurposed materials, and Blue Island Oyster Bar for fresh oysters. Or stop by Boulder Running Company to have your gait analyzed on one of the in-store treadmills and find your perfect shoe. Mess around on the incline path, take a free yoga class, or relax in a massage chair. This Cherry Creek location is the company's distribution center and biggest store, so the deals and services are topnotch. The original store in Boulder can credit its success to the exceptionally strong running culture of the Front Range. In fact, the Bolder Boulder 10k, held annually on Memorial Day, is one of the biggest foot races in the US.

Address 3000 E 1st Avenue, Denver, CO 80206, +1 (303) 388-3900,
www.shopcherrycreek.com | Getting there Bus 3, 3L, 83D, 83L to 1st Avenue &
University Boulevard | Hours Mon–Sat 10am–9pm, Sun 11am–7pm | Tip The sundial
at nearby Cranmer Park reminds you that not all technological innovations have moving
parts. Brilliantly simple, this head-high sundial is actually the park's second – the first was
inexplicably dynamited by vandals in 1965 (4300 E Third Avenue).

27 — Chipotle's Birthplace
The foil-wrapped revolution began here

The so-called Mission burrito was popularized in the Mission District of San Francisco but monetized in Denver. This hardy, handy burrito style is distinctive for its large size, use of rice, and easy-to-wrap steamed tortilla. University of Denver students responded enthusiastically to this ultimate hand food when the very first Chipotle opened here in July 1993. It only took one month before this restaurant location was selling more than 1,000 burritos a day. Almost 30 years later, the world can credit (blame?) these hungry pioneers for helping transform the humble burrito into the ubiquitous staple of mainstream American cuisine it has become. Today's Chipotle Mexican Grill serves 750,000 customers daily at approximately 2,000 locations worldwide, including France, Germany, and Canada.

Long before the rise of the Mission burrito, though, Taco Bell had already managed to ruin fast-food burritos by turning them into a cheap afterthought. But Chipotle has elevated this classic Mexican street food with fresh and healthy ingredients. In fact, Chipotle arguably set the standard for the success of other fast-food restaurant chains that were also founded in Denver, like Noodles & Co. and Smashburger. Quizno's, the chain of submarine sandwich shops, was started here in the 1980s.

In the Nahuatl language of Mesoamerica, a *chipotle* is a smoked or dried jalapeño pepper, and the brand incorporates Mayan glyphs to communicate its identity. This location (a former Dolly Madison ice cream shop) displays a large, silver Mayan glyph sculpture on the inside brick wall by the counter. The restaurant neighbors a recreational marijuana dispensary to create a beneficial loop of munchies and convenience. Jelly U across the street serves wicked gourmet donuts if you're more in the mood for something sweet. And the adjacent smoke shop offers discounts to students, of course.

Address 1644 E Evans Avenue, Denver, CO 80210, +1 (303) 722-4121, www.chipotle.com | **Getting there** Bus 21 to Evans Avenue & S High Street; RTD Rail to University of Denver (E, H Lines) | **Hours** Daily 10:45am–10pm | **Tip** Tacobe is like a Native American version of Chipotle. Frybread is on the menu, of course, but it's the bowls of heritage grains and fresh meats and vegetables that make it special (two Denver locations, www.tacobe.com).

28 City Center Park
Elijah McClain remembered

Peaceful protesters gathered at this modest park in Aurora in June of 2020 to mourn the memory of Elijah McClain, who was killed by local police. An effort at community healing, this solemn violin performance was broken up by Aurora police in riot gear, a violation that compounded the community trauma of McClain's death.

On August 24, 2019, Elijah McClain, just 23 years old, was walking home from a convenience store where he'd purchased an iced tea for his brother. Somehow the sight of a young black man walking on the sidewalk at night caused someone to call 911 and report a "suspicious" individual. When confronted by three police officers, McClain seemed confused and upset. This led police to subdue McClain physically and place him in a carotid chokehold, since banned by Aurora police. He was then injected with 500mg of ketamine, a powerful animal tranquilizer, and suffered cardiac arrest. McClain was pulled off life support days later. Shockingly, three Aurora Police Department officers were fired from the department after posting images on social media that mocked McClain's death.

The mundane nature of this Aurora park raises uncomfortable questions: Are we safe in our own neighborhoods? To what extent does skin color – or gender or sexual preference, for that matter – impact our safety? McClain was a massage therapist and known in the community for his volunteer work at animal shelters, where he'd play his violin for orphaned cats and dogs. His senseless death inspires Black Lives Matter activists to this day. Thankfully, the city of Aurora settled a wrongful death suit with McClain's family in 2021 for $15 million.

Aurora's City Center Park is a poignant place to remember McClain and just enjoy some greenery. The park is only 8.5 acres, but it has direct access to High Line Canal Trail, which bisects the city and is great for bike riding.

Address 14701 E Alameda Avenue, Aurora, CO 80012, www.auroragov.org | Getting there Bus 3, 3L, 6 to Alameda Avenue & S Sable Boulevard | Hours Unrestricted | Tip Artists Hiero Veiga and Thomas "Detour" Evans started the nationwide Spray Their Name mural project (www.spraytheirname.com) to honor victims of police violence. See huge paintings in Denver of George Floyd (E Colfax Avenue & High Street) and Breonna Taylor (2855 Walnut Street).

29 __ City Park Pavilion
19th-century boathouse

Originally completed as a boathouse in 1882 (and since rebuilt), the Spanish-style City Park Pavilion on Ferril Lake anchors City Park, the sentimental heart of Denver. This genteel greenbelt helped earn Denver the nickname Queen City of the Plains for being an oasis carved from the wilderness of the West. At 360 acres, today's City Park encompasses 15 athletic fields, 14 tennis courts, and two playgrounds, not to mention the Denver Museum of Nature & Science, the Denver Zoo, and several historic stone gateways. It's on the National Register of Historic Places in part because of the popular and public City Park Golf Course, in continuous operation since 1912.

Rent a paddle boat on Ferril Lake and shower yourself on hot days under the lake's careening fountain. Look for hunting heron and osprey. Or rent a bicycle (also from services in the park) and pedal to the corner of 17th Street and Colorado Avenue to find Shakespeare's Elm. This gnarly old tree was planted in 1916 and allegedly grown from a switch cut from a tree at William Shakespeare's gravesite at Holy Trinity Church, where the Bard was baptized and prayed, in Stratford-upon-Avon. Another park highlight is the Martin Luther King, Jr. Monument set among the roses in Sopris Gardens. The gigantic structure also honors equal-rights activists Gandhi, Rosa Parks, Fredrick Douglas, and Sojourner Truth.

As the crown jewel of local parks, City Park serves as a model for how green areas can uplift the community. Denver increased local sales tax in 2019 by .25% in order to raise funds for new park construction and park upkeep throughout the city. Parks are typically built in more affluent neighborhoods, but the City of Denver is making efforts to be more deliberate about constructing greenspaces in lower-income areas. Many of the flowers for the city's 150 other parks are grown in greenhouses here in City Park too.

Address 2001 Steele Street, Denver, CO 80205, www.denvergov.org | Getting there
Bus 20 to 17th Avenue & Esplanade | Hours Unrestricted | Tip When visiting the Denver
Museum of Nature & Science look for little red-capped elves painted in random places
throughout the 716,000-square-foot building (2001 Colorado Boulevard, www.dmns.org).

30 Cleo Parker Robinson Dance

Grande dame of dance companies

The nonprofit Cleo Parker Robinson Dance has achieved something akin to orthodoxy in this town. The lifelong work of the eponymous founder has helped move the African American experience from active repression to center stage. With its excellent ensemble, dance academy, theater, and education programs, this company is a cultural force that animates Five Points, once referred to as the Harlem of the West.

Similar to Alvin Ailey and his eponymous dance theater in New York, Denver-born Parker Robinson was a groundbreaking performer before turning to choreography. She is a graduate of George Washington High School (like beloved Denver singer Diane Reeves) and founded her dance troupe in 1970. She's a driving force for self-expression on stage and beyond, describing her own work best: "We use the universal language of dance to honor the African Diaspora, explore the human condition, champion social justice, unite people of all ages and races, and ultimately celebrate the complexity of life through movement."

Her father was a Black actor, and her mother a white musician. 1950s America was deadset against interracial marriage, and Parker Robinson experienced pervasive racism growing up. At age 10, she suffered a medical emergency in Dallas, Texas, but the local hospital was segregated and turned her away. Parker Robinson suffered kidney failure as a result and had a heart attack, nearly dying before finally receiving treatment. She chose to face this trauma by studying dance, which helped transform her emotional and physical pain.

The Cleo Parker Robinson Ensemble has performed at the Lincoln Center and toured internationally. Parker Robinson received a Kennedy Center Medal of Honor in 2005 and was inducted into the Colorado Women's Hall of Fame in 1989.

Address 119 Park Avenue W, Denver, CO 80205, +1 (303) 295-1759,
www.cleoparkerdance.org | Getting there Bus 28 to Clarkson Street & 22nd Avenue |
Hours See website for class schedule | Tip The strange, triangle-shaped building across the
street houses one of Denver's best Mexican restaurants, La Pasadita Inn. The owners are
from Durango, Mexico, and prepare the region's authentic cuisine (1959 Park Avenue W).

31 Clyfford Still Museum

Quiet terrasses syncopate modern art

The Clyfford Still Museum is a jaw-dropping tour de force of modern architecture by Brad Cloepfil. It's an intimidating cement square that squats next to the soaring exuberance of the Denver Art Museum. The building brilliantly accents Still's massive, abstract paintings. But you cannot miss the second-floor Terraces, surprising gems of studied restraint. These graceful, semi-outdoor spaces are covered by delicate latticework and lush lawns underfoot. In the perpetual bustle of the city, their quiet peace hides in plain sight.

The art of Clyfford Still (1904–1980) is a joyful juxtaposition to the museum building's mass. Light and color burst from Still's paintings and from select use of windows throughout the structure. The effect is a meditative masterpiece – a truly world-class art institution. There's approximately one decade's worth of art per room, which allows viewers to immerse themselves in the evolution of Still's iterative nature.

It's hard not to call the man a genius. He was ferociously singular yet somehow managed to speak in universal themes. He also had a sense of humor. Still's iron-clad will stipulated that his work would not be shown or studied after his death until a city committed to creating a collection "in perpetuity" to house it all. It took 31 years before his exacting demands were met.

The art establishment largely rejected Abstract Expressionism throughout the 1920s and 1930s, finally succumbing to the brilliant works of Clyfford Still, Jackson Pollock, Willem de Kooning, and others. Dubbed The Irascibles by the media, Abstract Expressionists insisted on "removing context" to express "inner comprehension," which confused most people. Still refused to name his paintings, not wanting to interfere with viewers' experience. The museum extravagantly indulges Still's vision, a total surrender that is immensely gratifying.

Address 1250 Bannock Street, Denver, CO 80204, +1 (720) 354-4880, www.clyffordstillmuseum.org | Getting there Bus 52 to Bannock Street & W 13th Avenue | Hours Wed–Sun 10am–5pm | Tip Across the street, the bright yellow Kirkland Museum of Fine & Decorative Art opens your eyes to the original, fun, and creative designs of everyday objects, like chairs by Frank Lloyd Wright and Eames, candlesticks by Dali, glasswork from Tiffany, and a dress designed by Andy Warhol (1201 Bannock Street, www.kirklandmuseum.org).

32 _ Cold War Horse
Environmental injustice remembered

The Rocky Flats Nuclear Weapons Plant in Arvada was one of the largest production facilities of its kind in the entire country before forcibly getting shut down in 1989. Approximately 70,000 plutonium triggers for America's nuclear-bomb arsenal were produced on site. Radioactive and deadly, weapons-grade plutonium has a half-life of 24,110 years, and the area's soil, water, and air was severely polluted for nearly 40 years, including leaking radioactive waste and plutonium fires. An FBI raid finally exposed the facility's many violations in the country's first-ever intergovernmental raid. The plant's operators eventually pled guilty to environmental crimes, leading to a 10-year, $7-billion cleanup operation.

Lost in the history of the Rocky Flats Nuclear Weapons Plant are the many workers who sacrificed their safety and health in service to their country. A class action lawsuit by sickened workers settled some claims, but the litany of cancers associated with former employees and their families is disturbing. Artist Jeffrey Gipe's father worked at the site for 20 years, and Gipe created *Cold War Horse* to commemorate these untold stories.

The colonization of the West is the saga of nature and industry colliding. And nothing symbolizes this fraught intersection better than the horse. Horses helped Europeans conquer and transform the West, and this statue's bright-red hazmat suit, black rubber boots, and gas mask make a wry statement about the lengths we're willing to go as Americans – and the justifications we employ – to make our violent history palatable.

Cold War Horse and its adjacent stone marker are effectively the only reminders of this area's troubled environmental history. Not without controversy, the statue was torn down by vandals just one month after its unveiling in 2015. Since reinstalled, this protest art honors the truth of what happened here.

Address 15650 Highway 72 & Coal Creek Canyon Road, Arvada, CO 80007 | **Getting there** Highway 36W to Sheridan Boulevard Exit, drive west on W 88th Avenue for about 4.5 miles. Statue is just west of Indiana Street. | **Hours** Unrestricted | **Tip** *Mustang* is the 32-foot-tall sculpture of a rearing blue horse at Denver International Airport. During its construction, this red-eyed monster toppled onto artist Luis Jiménez and killed him (8500 Peña Boulevard).

33__Confluence Kayak & Ski

Where outdoor athletes congregate

This outfitter is housed in a historic brick building once a hotel run by legendary Zang Brewery. This brewery drew from Denver's waters in the late 19th century, much like Coors does in Golden. Confluence Kayak & Ski is inspired by these same waters and caters to outdoor athletes with a wide array of summer and winter sports equipment and technical clothing. The exposed brick walls, stained glass, and weathered wood floors speak to the building's storied age. The indoor stairwell is a museum of old ski equipment, and the long bar top reminds of the building's origins. The immense mural of hikers on the building's north side hints at the toys inside.

In some ways, Confluence Park is the spiritual heart of Denver. First opened in 1975, this park is where the South Platte River and Cherry Creek join before meandering east to engorge the Missouri River – which in turn swells the Mississippi before eventually reaching the Gulf of Mexico. The abundance of water is why a town was built here on the dusty plains in the first place. After discovering gold, white settlers muscled in on local Arapahoe, who lived here and benefited from the rich hunting grounds of this water source. But thoughtless building in the floodplain led to a series of deadly floods over the next 100 years (1860s – 1960s). A $20-million restoration in the early 1970s rescued the South Platte from being a dumping ground for old cars, appliances, and toxic waste.

All kinds of events are held at Confluence Park today, including South Platte River Fest in June, when musicians, food trucks, kayakers, and SUP (stand-up paddleboard) enthusiasts congregate for good times. Confluence Kayaks is at the heart of this riverside community, offering boat rentals and instruction, plus repair. In winter, the staff flips the emphasis and transforms the building into a full-service ski and snowboard shop.

Address 2301 7th Street, Denver, CO 80211, +1 (303) 433-3676, www.confluencekayaks.com | Getting there Bus 28 to W 26th Avenue & Alcott Street | Hours Mon–Fri 10am–7pm, Sat 10am–6pm, Sun noon–5pm | Tip This REI Flagship Store is housed in the old Denver Tramway Powerplant. This beautiful brick edifice has soaring ceilings, with steel girders high enough for a legit indoor climbing wall (1416 Platte Street, www.rei.com).

34 __ Corner Beet

Vegetarian Valhalla in this life

It takes commitment to be an independent thinker. Vegetarianism is like that – a lifestyle choice for the body and the planet that cuts across the cultural grain and requires steadfastness. But being vegetarian can feel like a lonely crusade, which makes Corner Beet a welcoming haven. This vegetarian restaurant feeds a self-identified community with passion.

People with food sensitivities come here because the menu is 100 percent organic and somewhat customizable to accommodate various dietary needs. All the sauces and soups are nut-, gluten-, dairy-, and soy-free, and the fresh smoothies and cold-pressed organic juices are sensational. If you're ever going to try an ashwagandha, cinnamon, espresso, honey, and oat milk latte, this is the place.

While the popular vegetarian restaurant City O' City (206 E 13th Street) has a full bar and is open late, Corner Beet closes at 3:00 pm. It skews artisanal, proudly serves Grateful Bread and local produce exclusively. The covered outdoor seating area is sequestered from traffic with hay bales. There's a yoga studio next door. Corner Beet gives confidence that an entirely plant-based diet is possible. You could eat here every day and never miss meat.

The restaurant's hipster vibe is artistic and diverse. Servers have nose rings and ear gauges and wear dreadlocks and knitted sweaters. The clientele is diverse and quietly writes in journals, works on laptops, or chats intimately in plush chairs. The dark-stone bar top curves in a satisfying arc and has thoughtful hooks placed underneath to hang your insulated corduroy jackets and faux leather bags. People come here for nourishment of body and soul and to be seen on the scene. The music is loud, remixed jazz. The room is generously decorated with greenery, and a plant-lined shelf spans the large picture window. A bushy jade tree looks particularly happy. Hanging plants are everywhere.

Address 1401 N Ogden Street, Denver, CO 80218, +1 (720) 295-4447, www.cornerbeet.com |
Getting there Bus 15 to Colfax Avenue & Clarkson Street | Hours Mon–Fri 8am–4pm,
Sat 9am–4pm, Sun 9am–2pm | Tip Pete's Kitchen (1962 E Colfax Avenue,
www.petesrestaurants.com) is the absolute antithesis, which makes it just as wonderful.
Open 24 hours and ostensibly Greek, this is not a diner-about-being-a-diner. It's a diner.

35_Cruise Room
Denver's best martini

Modeled after HMS *Queen Mary*, this Denver treasure is softly bathed in trippy, pink lighting. The high ceilings, art deco wall panels, and large leather booths put you in the mood for a fabulous cocktail, preferably a martini. It's intimate and boozy and the kind of place that calls for dressing up. In fact, musician Jack White looks sharp in a retro-chic suit for the 2014 White Stripes music video "Would You Fight for My Love," filmed here (though the lighting was altered blue). He sits brooding at the bar, like some long lost star of film noir.

The Cruise room is just off the lobby of Denver's Grand Dame of Hotels, The Oxford, opened in 1891. The bar itself officially opened in 1933, the day after Prohibition ended, having already served as a clandestine speakeasy throughout the ban. It has been in continuous operation ever since. It's one of a number of speakeasy-styled joints that proudly serve the thirsty, including Williams & Graham (3160 Tejon Street, Denver) and the Green Russel (1422 Larimer Street, Denver).

In a funny twist not apparent until you think to notice, all bars in Colorado must serve food in addition to alcohol in order to receive a liquor license from the state. To meet regulations, the Cruise Room serves modest small plates from the hotel's Urban Farmer kitchen. For fantastic, locally sourced meat dishes with fresh vegetables, reserve a table at Urban Farmer "modern steakhouse." There's also an Amante coffee shop right out the front door, which serves authentic Italian espresso.

The Oxford is now on the National Register of Historic Places, but it had fallen into disrepair by the 1950s and was considered a flophouse. After several major restorations, today the Oxford is one of Denver's most elegant and best-located hotels. Just steps from Union Station and Wazee Street, it's both a portal to the past and to modern downtown Denver.

Address 1600 17th Street, Denver, CO 80202, +1 (303) 262-6070, www.theoxfordhotel.com |
Getting there Bus 0, 9, 15 20 to 18th & Blake Streets; RTD Rail to Union Station
(A, B Lines) | Hours Bar open daily 5 – 10pm | Tip Just around the corner from the Oxford
Hotel, Nativ Hotel is the country's first hotel to openly welcome cannabis use (1612 Wazee
Street, www.nativhotels.com).

36 Dairy Block

Drink your milk – and infused cocktails, too

The Windsor Dairy building was constructed in 1918 and provided Denver families with dairy products for generations into the seventies. Horse-drawn carriages would load up on glass milk bottles here and deliver them across the city. It's said the horses knew their routes so well they'd turn down streets and stop at drop-offs without command. The milk, butter, and cheese were processed in this building, but the cows grazed in southeast Denver, at today's Windsor Gardens, a retirement community and golf course. After growing wealthy, the dairy's founder transitioned into local government.

Interestingly, today's Front Range has a vibrant community of small dairy farmers (cow and goat), who sell through legal cowshare agreements. Pasteurization improves milk for transport and storage but also kills beneficial microbes and arguably reduces milk's nutritional value.

LoDo's industrial roots have long since been replaced by restaurants, bars, shops, and hotels, but developers pride themselves on keeping the brick-and-steel aesthetic. The Dairy Block, which incorporates the historic Windsor building, is a fine example. It's also emblematic of Denver's enthusiastic embrace of food halls: The Stanley, The Source, Central Market, and Union Station, to name a few. One of the many bars in the complex, Run for the Roses, is below street level and cultivates a Prohibition-era speakeasy feel. The crafted cocktails and vintage spirits are a time warp. At street level, the coffee at Huckleberry Roasters is exceptional. And upstairs, the 172-room Maven Hotel is pricey, but the loft-style rooms are unique.

Peruse the 16-venue Milk Market, with its numerous wine bars, whiskey and spirit bars, and restaurants. Then find a table in the outdoor, communal seating area in the narrow alley. Denverites are known for being chatty and sociable, especially in the warmer months.

Address 1800 Wazee Street, Denver, CO 80202, +1 (303) 309-4817, www.dairyblock.com | Getting there Bus 0, 9, 15 20 to 18th & Blake Streets; RTD Rail to Union Station (A, B Lines) | Hours See venues' websites | Tip The ART, a Hotel is an architectural marvel that goes out of its way to wow. The roof-top Garden Terrace alone is worth a visit (1201 Broadway, www.thearthotel.com).

37 _ Denver Beer Co.
The beer-centric lifestyle

Denver's award-winning Denver Beer Co. started in 2010, riding the wave of the city's devotion to quality suds to perfection. This microbrewery produces matchless beers that are creative and exceptionally well-executed, served in three taprooms in Denver and Arvada. Denver hosts the annual Great American Beer Festival, the nation's largest juried beer festival, and Colorado-based breweries are perennial winners. Denver Beer Co.'s Incredible Pedal IPA could not be more refreshingly hoppy and bitter, and their Tart Delight sour is citrusy sweet.

There are about 100 craft breweries in the Denver Metro Area (triple that across the Front Range). There's even a Great American Beer Store with a drive-thru on West Alameda Avenue. It all started with Tivoli Beer and Zang Brewing, two historic 19th-century, local brands that were advertised around town on murals that are still visible today. This legacy has spawned many success stories, including Blue Moon, probably the most nationally recognized beer produced in Denver. Colorado's most marketable politician, John Hickenlooper (Denver's former Mayor, former Colorado Governor, and current US Senator) built his success with Wynkoop Brewing, which he co-founded in the 1980s.

Denver has long attracted transplants for the relaxed lifestyle, sunny weather, affordability, and ample job opportunities. This translates to a fun-loving, beer-savvy public that seeks out original products. The proliferation of local breweries includes a strong class of women-owned breweries, too, like Grateful Gnome, Goldspot Brewing Company, Lady Justice Brewing, and Dry Dock Brewing.

Come hot summer days, the sociable outdoor beer garden of Denver Beer Co. on Platte Street is the place to be. A former auto mechanic, this taproom rolls up the garage doors and overflows onto the sidewalk. They even produce their beer with 100% solar power.

Address 1695 Platte Street, Denver, CO 80202, +1 (303) 433-2739, www.denverbeerco.com | Getting there Bus 28, 32, 44 to 15th & Platte Streets | Hours Mon–Thu 11am–10pm, Fri & Sat 11am–11pm, Sun 11am–9pm | Tip Arguably the nation's first regional beer to reach nationwide popularity, Coors (13th & Ford Streets, Golden, www.coorsbrewerytour.com) has grown into a mega-factory that seems to take up half the town. Bonus: The brewery tours include free beer!

38 Denver Mint

The actual coin of the realm

Colorado's 19th-century gold and silver mines created a surplus of precious metals, and the Denver Mint was constructed to process these metals into coins for safe transport, commerce, and better accounting. Founded as an assay office in 1863, today's Denver Mint has been in constant operation since 1906. This mint churns out approximately 40 million coins a day – about 8 billion annually. On a tour, you will see the various machines whirring at full tilt. This is one of only four mints in the country and produces all the coins for the entire western United States. Coins manufactured in Denver are stamped with a tiny "D" just behind the President's neck.

The US Mint was founded in 1792 and is one of the nation's oldest federal agencies. In fact, the original mint in Philadelphia was the first federal building constructed under the Constitution. The US Mint was also the first federal agency to hire women in 1795! The Colorado Gold Rush started in 1859 when the Front Range was still part of Kansas Territory. The railroad lines built to haul gold from the mountains played a major role in creating the economic base of Denver. The influx of miners led to the incorporation of Denver itself and to Colorado statehood in 1876, earning the nickname Centennial State.

The Mint's slab-like building is no architectural marvel, but it looks appropriately fortified for a place where coins are minted. It's said to be designed after a Medici-family palazzo in Italy, but, really, it's just a square block. If you want to experience more gratifying Italian-inspired architecture in Denver, go to the 16th Street Mall and gaze up at the Daniels and Fisher Tower. Both buildings are on the National Register of Historic Places, but the tower is modeled after the Campanile di San Marco, in Venice, Italy. Monuments celebrating god will always outshine cenotaphs to the god of money.

Address 320 W Colfax Avenue, Denver, CO 80204, +1 (303) 405-4761, www.usmint.gov | Getting there Bus 16 W Colfax Avenue & Elati Street | Hours See website for tour schedule | Tip The Money Museum at the Federal Reserve Bank of Kansas City has exhibits on counterfeiting, famous collections, and how the Federal Reserve helps stabilize the economy (1020 16th Street, www.kansascityfed.org/moneymuseum).

39 __ Deer Trail

The world's first rodeo town

Denver has hosted the National Western Stock Show and its professional rodeo since 1906. The annual cattle drive through the streets of Denver, which kicks off the two-week event, is emblematic of the city. The sight of longhorns and horseback cowboys in January clacking the cobblestones of Wazee Street pulls the heartstrings of any Denverite. It's a little-known fact that Colorado actually originated the sport of rodeo itself.

Just 50 miles east of Denver, Deer Trail (population: 519) is surrounded by ranchland. Cowboys have herded cattle on this swath of the Great Plains since the mid-19th century, and in 1869 Deer Trail hosted the first competitive rodeo event ever held in the US. (Yes, Pecos, Texas, and Prescott, Arizona, make similar claims, but documents indicate Deer Trail was likely the first.) A group of local cowboys needed to settle a bet: Who was best at breaking wild horses quickly and efficiently? A competition that tests ranch work skills became known as a rodeo ("to surround" in Spanish). Americans learned how to cowboy from Mexicans and adopted many Spanish words to describe the craft, like *remuda* (horse herd) and lariat (rope). The term "buckaroo" comes from *vaquero*, Spanish for cowboy.

The Deer Trail Rodeo is held in July, but a visit any time of year is blast into the past. Hook a boot heel on a fence at the rodeo arena, or wander the sleepy downtown area. An ever-present, lonely wind whistles between the dusty buildings here. The Deer Trail Pioneer Historical Museum showcases items from the area's raw-boned ranching and homesteading past. The informative displays are housed in an old train depot, original log cabin, and a one-room schoolhouse. For incredible cuts of beef and pork, stop at Deer Trail Meat Company. Or try the wild game, lamb, and goat at Deer Trail Custom Cuts. Both butchers source all the animals locally.

Address 1900 2nd Avenue, Deer Trail, CO 80105, +1 (303) 769-4464,
www.townofdeertrail.colorado.gov | Getting there By car, take I-70 to Exit 328 towards
Deer Trail | Hours Unrestricted | Tip The ProRodeo Hall of Fame hosts an annual
induction ceremony and, of course, a small rodeo. The excellent historic and educational
displays put this American-bred sport into perspective (101 Pro Rodeo Drive, Colorado
Springs, www.prorodeohalloffame.com).

40 Eben G. Fine Park

Float. Hitchhike. Repeat.

Named for one of the founding fathers of Boulder, Eben G. Fine Park is the starting point for the kooky warm-weather tradition of floating Boulder Creek. Much like the revelers at Confluence Park (see ch. 33), Front Range locals, students, and fun hogs anxiously await for the weather to get warm in May and for Boulder Creek to swell with spring snowmelt. The weekend flotillas are a party crowd. People float downriver in all manner of watercraft – everything from innertubes and inflatable flamingos to sleeping pads and old canoes. (There's also an actual kayak course for real river rats.)

Affectionately known to locals as Mr. Boulder, Eben Givens Fine (1865–1957) was a pharmacist in Boulder for decades and a mainstay of the Chamber of Commerce. He helped raise funds to build Boulder's venerable Boulderado Hotel, which opened in 1909, and traveled widely to promote the wonders of the Front Range. Fun fact: Boulder High, opened in 1876, is the oldest high school in Colorado.

On hot summer weekends, the atmosphere on the creek definitely gets rowdy. Whooping crowds float down the water to the Boulder Public Library and then shuttle cars or hitchhike back upriver to the park. Float, hitchhike, repeat. There are thoughtfully placed stonework cairns along the creek, with placid areas for swimming and safe areas for launching watercraft.

Multiple bridges cross Boulder Creek between the park and the library and make for great viewing. There's also an annual Tube to Work Day in July (www.tubetoworkday.com), when people dress up in business suits and ostensibly "float to work" *en masse.*

Eben G. Fine Park has a big lawn for lounging under immense cottonwoods, creek-side picnic tables, a playground, and convenient public restrooms. The Boulder Creek Path, a paved path for meandering that accesses the mountain trails west of town, traverses the park, too.

Address 101 Arapahoe Avenue, Boulder, CO 80302, +1 (303) 413-7200, www.bouldercolorado.gov/locations/eben-g-fine-park | Getting there Bus NB 1, NB 2 to Canyon Boulevard & Pearl Street | Hours Unrestricted | Tip Surfers head to River Run Park when the Army Corps of Engineers releases water from Chatfield Reservoir. Hydraulic wave-shaping machinery is also employed to create surfable waves (2101 W Oxford Avenue, Sheridan, www.endlesswaves.net/waves/river-run-park).

41 Erico Motorsports

European motorcycles as art

The meticulously restored, candy-apple red 1956 Moto Guzzi Lodola on display at Erico Motorsports would hold its own in any museum in the world. But this masterpiece of two-wheeled, no-door engineering is just one of many classic motorcycles and scooters showcased, most of which are mounted to a giant wall rack. Owner John Beldock turned his passion for wrenching and racing into a business 25 years ago and has made it a priority to root the culture of his shop in motorcycle history.

The post-World War II production boom in Europe drew inspiration from racing and commuting. Europeans value high-speed touring motorcycles and low-speed, efficient scooters for commuting and parking. The seminal models at Erico Motorsports represent the heritage of development that produced modern European motorcycles.

Erico is the Denver retailer for Great Britain-manufactured Triumph and Italian-made Moto Guzzi and Ducati. They also sell Vespa, Piaggio, and Aprilia scooters, plus Erico custom-designed bikes. Think: stripped-down café racers, ferocious Grand Prix-inspired street racers, and cute *Roman Holiday* scooters. There's a used selection too.

Conversely, American pop culture typically stereotypes motorcycle riders as Harley-Davidson-driving tough guys, largely derived from Marlon Brando's *The Wild One* and Dennis Hopper's *Easy Rider*. Heck, even *Dawg the Bounty Hunter*, Denver's native son Duane Chapman, was a member of the Devil's Disciples, an "outlaw" biker gang. After serving time in federal prison for a drug deal gone bad and an alleged killing, he's milked the tough-guy image in the cable netherworld ever since.

Visit Erico Motorsports' 1930s brick warehouse and former metal fabrication plant to shop for your next ride or just to admire these iconic bikes. And check out the padded leather riding gear and boots. Despite Colorado's insane no-helmet law, Erico sells helmets, too.

Address 2855 Walnut Street, Denver, CO 80205, +1 (303) 308-1811,
www.ericomotorsports.com | Getting there Bus 44 to Larimer & 28th Streets | Hours
Tue–Sat 10am–5pm | Tip Flip the riding-philosophy script and check out the low and
slow cruisers at Sun Harley-Davidson, Colorado's oldest and largest Harley dealership
(8855 Pearl Street, www.denverharley.com).

42 Essence Studio
Custom-crafted perfumes

Everyone's body has a unique smell, which is one reason why scents register so differently on different people. Our sense of smell bypasses the cerebral cortex and touches something mysteriously primal. In addition to a line of signature scents, Essence Studio creates bespoke, or custom, perfume blends that match body odor and personal taste with natural oils to fine-tune this internal olfactory compass. Owner Dawn Spencer Horowitz is a trained aromatherapist and has been in the perfume business for 30 years. She has experienced synesthesia since childhood; numbers appear as colors to her. She's developed this perceptual phenomenon one step further by transforming colors into smells.

Spencer Horowitz speaks of perfume blending in poetic terms, referencing architecture, music, and texture. She describes her work as "scented storytelling." A fragrance consultation (or "Smell and Tell") involves smelling the client's skin then presenting various oils that match well. She interviews clients about their emotional needs and builds a personalized scent for that client alone. These scents can also be blended into body washes, massage oils, and bubble baths. She almost exclusively uses natural oils derived from plants, only occasionally using synthetic oils manufactured by chemists to add "structure" to her blends.

There are typically two kinds of people who wear perfumes – the signature wearer sticks with one scent, and the wardrobe wearer likes to change scents. Some people like to be recognized by their friends and family by the scent they wear, while others use scents as a personal motivator or mood enhancer. Spencer Horowitz hosts events at museums, where she crafts perfume blends to match paintings. She also offers perfumery classes. A master at crafting scents "to make an impact on your life," she'll find a perfume that's perfect for you.

Address 4593 N Broadway, Boulder, CO 80304, +1 (720) 563-0344, www.dshperfumes.com |
Getting there Bus FF1 to Downtown Boulder Station, then SKIP bus to Broadway &
Yarmouth Avenue | Hours Tue 11am–5pm, Wed–Fri noon–5pm, Sat noon–4pm |
Tip Wntr Rose Apothecary carries exquisite body care products and natural perfumes
(47 W 11th Avenue, www.wntrroseapothecary.com).

43 Fairy Doors
Gateways to another world

It says something about a city when the mayor challenges city council members to compete on beautification projects and makes funds available for local artists to work their magic. This is what Mayor Michael Hancock did with the Imagine 2020 grant program. One result is *Fairy Doors of South Pearl Street,* Platte Park's whimsical set of tiny entrance façades to the homes of fairy folk.

Three dimensional, with little awnings, windows, and ornate entrances, the fairy doors inspire a kind of reverence. People leave tokens (pennies, flowers, shells, or "anything shiny") to please these guardian spirits. There's a map online that shows where to locate the doors, and the local merchants encourage this frivolity. You can see a total of 17 fairy doors scattered throughout the South Pearl Street shopping district.

There's even a fairy door on the Denver City & County Building across Civic Center Park from the State Capitol (see ch. 65). Many are designed to look like the businesses they adorn, like the one at Duffeyroll Bakery Café. Others are more fantastical, and all are completely charming.

The belief in the *tompte*, a mercurial little gnome, is particularly Scandinavian. Old-school Swedish farmers still place bowls of porridge in their barns to keep the creatures happy and out of mischief. Usually invisible, these gnome-like beings are associated with specific places and regarded as a kind of ancestral protector spirit. Thanks to the many Scandinavians of the Upper Midwest, this folklore has taken root there. Fairy doors first showed up in Ann Arbor, Michigan, in the early 1990s before spreading west to Colorado.

If your South Pearl Street fairy hunt stirs an appetite, beeline for Park Burger (1890 Pearl Street) or Platt Park Brewing Co. (1875 Pearl Street) across the street. Both are excellent eateries and host adorable fairy doors, of course.

Address S Pearl Street, Denver, CO 80210, www.spearlstfairydoors.weebly.com, spearlfairies@gmail.com | Getting there Bus 12 to S Pearl Street & Louisiana Avenue | Hours Unrestricted | Tip Stella's Gourmet Coffee & Such slings the attitude and exceptional coffee from a lovely old brick home. There's a hidden fairy door there too (1476 S Pearl Street, www.stellascoffe.com).

44 Far East Center

Never run out of soy sauce cups again

Denver is a blue-collar town at its heart. One of the major arteries, Federal Boulevard on the west side of town, is the kind of unglamorous, urban thoroughfare where locals from lower-income communities shop – and tourists typically avoid. But Federal teems with ethnic character, souped-up cars, and hand-painted signs advertising steaming bags of fresh-roasted Hatch chilis. Many of the Asian and Mexican businesses along the road don't even pretend to cater to English speakers, like the *llanteras*, or tire service stores. Why is there a restaurant called PHO 555 that's literally across the street from another restaurant called PHO 86? And these are a short walk from a third, seemingly identical, Vietnamese *pho* restaurant. Rich, brothy soup is popular in these parts.

The brightly painted, pagoda-shaped entry arch at the Far East Center is wonderfully out of place. The Asian businesses exclusively featured in this little mall are anchored by Little Saigon Supermarket, a Vietnamese market with a dizzying array of Asian foods, products, and fresh produce. Truong An Far East Asian Gifts has aisle upon aisle of shelves jam-packed with Chinese herbs, anime characters, jade Buddhas, good luck charms, cutlery, and much more. The center also has two Vietnamese restaurants (with mandatory fish tanks), and the humble China Jade Restaurant, which serves Denver's best dim sum. For good measure, there's an Asian-owned law firm with translation services, a hair salon, and a cell phone repair shop.

The Far East Center may remind you of San Francisco's Chinatown – it's a little run down, and shop owners are not particularly outgoing. But the deals to be had are incredible. You can buy handfuls of incense for pocket change, and getting lost in aisles of unfamiliar objects you don't need is fun. You may find yourself buying a rice cooker or a colorful peacock feather.

Address 333 S Federal Boulevard, Denver, CO 80219, +1 (303) 936-5004, www.littlesaigondenver.com | Getting there Bus 30, 31 to S Federal Boulevard & W Alameda Avenue | Hours Mon–Fri 9am–5:30pm, Sat 10am–4:30pm | Tip Domo is a country-style Japanese restaurant with outdoor garden seating. The food could not be more authentic, as is the neighboring aikido dojo (1365 Osage Street, www.domorestaurant.com).

45__Folsom Custom Skis

Built to last and shred

Even the most casual weekend warrior can see their skiing improve by riding skis that are hand-built to match their body. Folsom Custom Skis designs and engineers boards according to skier height, weight, and ability, thereby earning themselves darling-status from the ski-industry press since the company opened for business in 2008. Folsom produces functional works of art that enhance the on-mountain experience. You can even select from a wide array of top sheet designs or submit one yourself. Their mini-factory is incomparable – a fully catered ski shopping experience.

Building skis is extremely technical, and these guys are master craftsmen. The team builds for performance and durability, fine-tuning every aspect of ski shape and incorporating a mix of space-age materials. Each pair of skis has a two-year "satisfaction-guaranteed" warranty, basically unheard of with mass-produced skis. Wait patiently for three to five weeks for delivery, then it's off to the mountains! Folsom sells models of stock skis as well.

Colorado is central to the ski industry, and the Folsom staff, though not entirely Denver-born-and-raised, got here as fast as they could. It's the highest-elevation state in the nation, with 54 mountains 14,000 feet or higher and 637 more between 13,000 and 13,999 feet. The US operations of ski-lift manufacturer Leitner-POMA are based in Grand Junction, and many ski brands like Spyder and Flylow are in the Front Range.

Broadway can actually lay claim to another custom ski maker just down the street: Meier Skis "handmade skis from Colorado trees." And Colorado is flush with excellent local ski brands, like Faction, High Society, Liberty, and Fat-ypus. Golden-based Icelantic Skis has been resourceful enough to partner with the City of Denver to host an annual concert at Red Rocks Amphitheater in January. You can't go wrong shopping for skis in Denver.

Address 7100 Broadway, Units 1K & 1L, Denver, CO 80221, +1 (303) 248-3418, www.folsomskis.com, info@folsomskis.com | **Getting there** Bus 8 to Broadway & 70th Avenue | **Hours** Mon–Fri 8am–6pm | **Tip** Never Summer has been making snowboards in Denver since 1991. They are a standard bearer for the industry and have great deals at their outlet store (3838 Eudora Way, www.neversummer.com).

46 Forney Museum
Planes, trains, automobiles, and more

Amelia Earhart was the first female pilot to fly across the Atlantic Ocean in 1932, having already completed the feat as a passenger in 1928. She was also the first person to fly from Hawaii to California and the first woman to fly solo across North America and back. Her aviation skills and bravery made her a world-wide celebrity. Earhart further indulged her thrill seeking by purchasing the 1923 Kissel Model 45 "Gold Bug" Speedster on display at the Forney Museum of Transportation. She paid $1,895 ($31,000 in today's dollars) for this yellow three-speed convertible and reportedly drove it like a demon.

Earhart nicknamed her car the Yellow Peril and drove it from California to Boston. Contemporary reports from family and friends uniformly describe her as a talented driver, if fast and possibly reckless. Earhart went on to own several other cars, but the 61-horsepower Gold Bug was said to be her favorite for having set her free in a male-dominated society. Today, she's regarded as a feminist icon for her aviation adventures and business savvy.

The founder of the Forney Museum, welding-equipment inventor J. D. Forney (1905–1986), had a sweet spot for Kissel vehicles, too, having traded a Ford Model T for a Kissel touring car while still in high school. He purchased Earhart's dilapidated car in 1960 and completed a full restoration.

Though most of the museum's more than 600 vehicles didn't have famous owners, their unique places in transportation history make these electric-powered drag racing motorcycles, wooden bicycles, trolley cars, helicopters, trains, cars, snowmobiles, and more just as fascinating. On a wall by the three cases of polished hood ornaments is also a nice display honoring Bessie Coleman, in 1921 the first Black person and first Native American to earn a pilot's license in the US. Both Coleman and Earhart died in tragic plane crashes.

Address 4303 Brighton Boulevard, Denver, CO 80216, +1 (303) 297-1113, www.forneymuseum.org | Getting there Bus 48 to Brighton Boulevard & 43rd Street | Hours Mon & Thu–Sat 10am–5pm, Sun noon–5pm | Tip Formerly Lowry Airforce Base, Wings over the Rockies Air & Space Museum has a mind-blowing collection of historical military aircraft (7711 E Academy Boulevard, www.wingsmuseum.org).

47___Four Mile House
Homesteading time capsule

Built in 1859, Four Mile House is Denver's oldest standing structure. The original log cabin, two-stories with a storage cellar, has siding now, and subsequent brick additions have expanded the footprint. It's a time capsule of Victorian aspirations to make good in the wilderness. A mirror in the study is said to reflect the ghost of a child. The building served as a stagecoach stop, earning its name for being four miles northwest of Denver. Travelers were strictly separated by gender, and the men were served Taos Lightning whiskey, cut with gunpowder (and sometimes deadly), and gambled into the night.

The house is now part of 12-acre Four Mile Historic Park, though the original farm spanned 600 acres. The soft bleating of goats mixes pleasantly with the city's hum, and every fourth Sunday, historic reenactors display crafts, including spinning wool from the property's Angora goats. One of the original owners was a master beekeeper and sold thousands of pounds of honey and beeswax annually. Look for honey and beeswax products in the gift shop.

On the banks of Cherry Creek, Four Mile House offered services to travelers following the Cherokee Trail, a northern offshoot of the Santa Fe Trail. The pioneers heading for Denver were pursuing gold and silver booms and taking advantage of the Homestead Act of 1862. Approximately 500,000 settlers traveled the overland routes across the Great Plains between 1840–1880. When the railroad arrived in Denver in 1870, Four Mile House slowly reverted to being a homestead and farm.

In the cellar, you can see the family's communal casket. Polished wood with copper trim and frosted glass, it was used for generations. Once the deceased reached the cemetery, they would be transferred to a simple coffin for burial. The sitting room displays an ornate mourning wreath made from woven hair of these deceased loved ones.

Address 715 Forest Street, Glendale, CO 80246, +1 (720) 865-0800, www.fourmilepark.org, info@fourmilepark.org | Getting there Bus 46 to S Cherry Street & Cherry Creek S Drive | Hours Wed–Sun 10am–4pm | Tip Actor Bill Paxton (*Apollo 13, Tombstone, Weird Science*) could also swing a hammer, thanks to his family's lumber business founded in 1914, Frank Paxton Lumber Company. The building's intricate wood trusses look like the vaulted ceiling of a church (4837 Jackson Street, www.paxtonwood.com).

48_ Ghost Rider Boots
Footwear as heirlooms

Leather craftsmanship can make the difference between life and death on horseback or doing ranch work. Be it a saddle, a harness, or a humble pair of boots, rough work requires heavy-duty equipment. And what's more basic – and critical – than good footwear? Nothing. That's what bootmaker Mickey Mussett would tell you when you visit Ghost Rider Boots. Mussett likes to tell stories, and you'll enjoy listening.

His first professional career was in advertising, but Mussett found his calling making cowboy boots of fine leather. "I'm an artist," he says plainly. "I live for making people happy and getting them exactly what they want. That's the best part of the job." And in 18 years, he's "never not had a boot to build," so he must be doing something right.

Visits to his garage-based shop are by appointment only, and Mussett lavishes attention on his customers. "Governor John Hickenlooper sat right there under the cow," he says, offhandedly. Everything in the shop feels well-worn and ancient. Many of his wood-handled hand tools are not even produced any more. Like his boots, the tools for building them are made to last. The dusty sewing machines and heel grinder are pushing 100 years old.

Mussett takes enormous pride in his ability to hand tool custom designs into the leather and inlay exotic leather patterns onto his boots. Whatever the customer wants, the customer gets – for a price, of course. Mussett won't reveal what he charges, but his boots are a great investment because they'll last many decades. Just resole them when the time comes.

After measuring and consulting on style, Mussett works on each pair of boots for approximately 80 hours. Customers choose from an array of leathers: elephant, ostrich, lizard, alligator, cow, and more. And each stitch is threaded with the "spirit of the Old West." The cowboy way is a living heritage in Mussett's hands.

Address 890 Grape Street, Denver, CO 80220, +1 (303) 284-7744, www.ghostriderboots.com | **Getting there** Bus 10 to 9th Avenue & Dahlia Street | **Hours** By appointment only | Tip Hill Brothers Boots sells work boots, western boots, and Carhartt clothing. That's it. A former stagecoach stop and next to a former lumber yard, this building has been here since trolleys ran down Broadway (1901 S Broadway).

49_ Governor's Residence
A mansion home to Colorado's first family

Affectionately known as Colorado's Home, the Cheesman-Evans-Boettcher Mansion covers nearly a full city block. It was built as a private residence in 1908, one of the many large, single-family homes that formed the exclusive Capitol Hill neighborhood – this one ringed by wrought iron fencing and ivy-covered brick walls. Step inside between the white columns for public tours. Ornate tapestries and dark-wood grandfather clocks abound. The second and third floors are the private quarters of the so-called first family. The wall of photos and portraits devoted to the state's first ladies now has a welcome 21st-century addition: first husband Marlon Reis, Governor Jared Polis' husband.

Walter Scott Cheesman, the man who designed the building in collaboration with his daughter, first traveled to Denver from Chicago by oxcart in 1861. He ran a drugstore business with his brother and later married a wealthy heiress. Cheesman died before seeing the building finished, and his widow remarried an Evans (Colorado royalty) and completed Cheesman's vision. The final private owners, the Boettcher family, donated the property to the State of Colorado in 1959, and it's been the residence for Colorado's sitting governors ever since. The Boettchers also purchased the magnificent Waterford crystal chandelier, which originally lit the East Room of the White House during President Grant's administration (1869–1877).

The South-facing Palm Room may be the building's most distinctive feature. The glass crescent of floor-to-ceiling window panels opens onto a rose garden with views of Pikes Peak. The room's glittering white marble can be blinding in the sun. The other mansions in this neighborhood are no less ostentatiously gorgeous, including the Grant-Humphreys Mansion next door, which can be rented for private events. Quiet Governor's Park and playground separates the properties.

Address 400 E 8th Avenue, Denver, CO 80203, +1 (303) 866-5344, www.governor-residence.colorado.gov | Getting there Bus 6 to 8th Avenue & Logan Street | Hours See website for tour schedule | Tip Denver Public Library's Central Library location is a glorious travesty of a building – a collision of shapes that's all the more cacophonous being across the street from the brilliant Denver Art Museum (10 W 14th Avenue, www.denverlibrary.org).

50__Grizzly Rose

Boot scootin' heaven

Two mechanical bulls? Check. Line dancing? Check. Hot bartenders in chaps? Check. Welcome to the Grizzly Rose, a real Western honky-tonk, with live music five days a week. The floating hardwood dancefloor is a massive 2,400 square feet, so you and your posse will have all the room you need to show off your moves.

Self-billed as a saloon and dance emporium, the "Rose" opened in 1989 and is the last big holdout of Denver's once-thriving western bar scene. The building has several bars to keep the drinks flowing fast. The Rose gets packed and raucous, especially on Thursday nights when women drink for free. But it has a family vibe, too. Kids flock the dancefloor on Sundays, when all ages are welcome, and most shows are open to 18-year-olds and up. Youngsters learn how to line dance here with their parents and then loyally return as adults. The free dance lessons on Wednesday nights keep people coming back.

Everyone from Joan Jett and Taylor Swift to Willie Nelson and Waylon Jennings have played here. Garth Brooks and Toby Keith basically launched their careers at the Rose, and the venue remains fully committed to booking "both kinds of music" – Country *and* Western. You'll even see touring musicians at the bar on their off nights. The place is a Denver landmark.

When your feet get tired of dancing, test your strength on the punching bag game, or retreat to the well-ventilated indoor smoking area and bond with diehard Marlboro Men. In the way, *way* back, there's an area for practicing roping, and it wouldn't be a honky-tonk without pool tables – five, to be exact.

The Rose hits full stride in January when the annual National Western Stock Show comes to town. The joint gets filled to capacity, with lines out the door. Belly up to the bar and argue over cowboy hat brims (flat, broad, or narrow) and cowboy boot toes (pointed, rounded, or square).

Address 5450 Lincoln Street, Denver, CO 80216, +1 (303) 295-1330, www.grizzlyrose.com |
Getting there Bus 8 to Lincoln Street & 54th Avenue | **Hours** Thu–Sat 6pm–2am,
Wed & Sun 6pm–midnight | **Tip** In the spirit of the venerable International Gay Rodeo
Association, Charlie's (900 E Colfax Avenue, www.charliesdenver.com) is basically the
Grizzly Rose for gay guys…and drag queens. Yeehaw!

51 Gusterman Silversmiths

Keeping an ancient trade alive

Started by a Swedish immigrant, Gusterman Silversmiths is the last traditional silversmith in Denver. Mary Eckels started working here in 1970 and bought the business from the daughters of the original owners in 1978. Today's shop in the Bull & Bear Courtyard of Larimer Square is within 50 feet of the original storefront. A little silver bell tinkles your arrival as you walk through the heavy wooden door.

Eckels and her team of longtime employees pride themselves on customer service. She's known for producing original designs and custom orders, like wedding rings, pendants, and earrings. One of the display cases is dedicated to original Gusterman-molded rings and fine jewelry. Gusterman Silversmiths is also known for making challises for local churches and cathedrals. But it's repair work that "pays the rent when business is slow," says Eckels. "I like seeing special pieces transferred to the next generation." Silverware mangled by kitchen disposals is an all-too common restoration.

There's a large print above the shop entrance that's a reproduction of a 15th-century German woodcut depicting a silversmithing shop. Eckles points out that many of the techniques employed by the workers in the picture have not changed in over 500 years. You can see the same tools on her two cluttered worktables: pliers, files, magnifying lenses, hammers, chasing tools, pitch bowls, and anvils.

Walk through the Kettle Arcade archway into the Bull & Bear Courtyard, and you'll discover a quiet, shady canyon of brick and wrought iron. The benches in front of Gusterman Silversmiths seem custom-made for eating ice cream. But this homely storefront belies the fact filmmaking royalty from around the globe has Gusterman work in their homes – Eckels has made the silver medallion awarded to winners at the Telluride Film Festival for the last 40 years.

Address 1418 Larimer Street, Denver, CO 80202, +1 (303) 629-6927, www.gustermans.com | Getting there Bus 6, 43 to Larimer & 14th Streets | Hours Tue—Sat 10am—6pm | Tip Walk back towards Larimer Square, and under the Kettle Arcade archway, you'll see a staircase to subterranean Wednesday's Pie Shop. Pass through the swinging doors at the back of the shop and into Green Russell, a Prohibition-era speakeasy (1422 Larimer Street, www.greenrussell.com).

52 Hammond's Candies

Handmade treats for the hands-free age

Founded in Denver in 1920, Hammond's Candies was started with a singular purpose: hand-made fine candies. The industrial mechanization that's occurred in food production over the intervening 100 years is truly mind boggling, but Hammond's has not changed one iota. They even use some of their original candy-making machines, already old when purchased from a defunct competitor in the 1920s.

Unlike the rascally Willie Wonka, this company does not hoard golden tickets. Visitors are welcome for free factory tours six days a week on the half hour. After a 10-minute video about the arcana of candy making, you're escorted into a long hallway with banks of windows. There, you can ogle at "the kitchen" before being handed samples and ushered into the candy shop.

Hammond's is best known for making candy canes and candy sticks (no hook) in every color combination and flavor imaginable, from traditional peppermint, cinnamon, and butterscotch to tie-dyed cotton candy, caramel apple, and even filled ones, like birthday cake canes filled with frosting and raspberry canes filled with chocolate.

The candy makers work on metal tables fitted lengthwise with hooded propane flames to keep the brightly colored blobs of sugar malleable. The mounds are pulled, stretched, twisted, rolled, and cut with elegant precision. You may find yourself staring hypnotically at the efficient chefs and candy makers working the bright colors.

Kitchen temperatures hover at 100°F degrees, and the staff must wear double-layered gloves when handling the hot, taffy-like sugar mounds. In other words, making candy by hand is hard work. The now-obscure Honey Ko Kos (chocolates topped with shredded coconut) were Hammond's first breakthrough success, but today the company makes every candy variety imaginable – 4,000 pounds a day and 10 million pieces a year – and ships them all over the world.

Address 5735 Washington Street, Denver, CO 80216, +1 (303) 333-5588, www.hammondscandies.com | Getting there Bus 8 to Logan Court & 57th Avenue | Hours Mon–Sat 9am–4pm | Tip There is never not a line at the silo-sized milk jug of Little Man Ice Cream, serving up scoops and helping the world (2620 16th Street, www.littlemanicecream.com).

53　Hudson Gardens

A day in the country in the city

Listening to the mellow hum of 100,000 bees can be intoxicating (as long as you're not deathly allergic). You won't find many community apiaries in Denver, and this collection of about 25 beehives in Littleton does more than produce honey and beeswax. The enormous concentration of vibrating wings creates a soothing acoustic bath. Hudson Gardens actively promotes pesticide-free beekeeping and pollinator gardens, of course, and hosts beekeeping programs and educational tours. The apiary is also incorporated into the beekeeping classes led by the Colorado Beekeepers Association. Study up, and bring home the buzz.

Hudson Gardens and Events Center, the generous public bequest of King and Evelyn Hudson, is a 30-acre paradise of delicate gardens, lily-filled ponds, and whimsical sculptures. The profusion of flowers, herbs, and cottonwoods is a welcome burst of natural life in suburbia. The center's gentle trails wend past shaded ponds, and all seem to lead to the Nixon's Coffeehouse.

The Hudsons opened a restaurant here in 1942 and ran it together in an old log building for 20 years. Country Kitchen quickly became famous for offering its patrons a smorgasbord of 70 dishes for $1.25 a head. The restaurant was especially popular for its fried chicken, scalloped potatoes, and Swedish rye bread. *Life* magazine even mentioned the restaurant in a travel issue featuring roadside attractions.

King Hudson was originally a dentist and an attorney. He moved to Denver in order to serve in the Army dental corps at Fort Logan. He would quit the Army to follow Evelyn's lead and open the Country Kitchen. The couple grew many of the vegetables and lettuces for the restaurant on the property and expressly wanted the public to enjoy the natural beauty they adored. The Hudson Gardens and Events Center opened to the public here on the east banks of the South Platte River in 1996.

Address 6115 S Santa Fe Drive, Littleton, CO 80120, +1 (303) 797-8565, www.hudsongardens.org | Getting there Bus 29, 36, 59 to W Church Avenue & S Santa Fe Drive | Hours Daily 7am – 7pm | Tip To Bee or Not to Bee is the premier beekeeping store in the Denver Metro Area (8280 W Coalmine Avenue, Littleton, www.tobeeornottobee.us).

54 International Church of Cannabis

The burning bush of holy sacraments

Marijuana has not replaced the columbine as Colorado's Official Flower (yet), but the International Church of Cannabis would likely endorse the idea. The congregation here calls themselves Elevationists and gathers for "celebrations" to consume the "sacred flower," aka fat, fragrant marijuana buds. Their goal is to reveal the "best version of themselves, discover their creative voice, and enrich their community with the fruits of that creativity." Yes, this is an open-minded town.

Humanity has ritually consumed various plant medicine drugs to expand consciousness throughout its history and across the globe. The services here are staid and respectful. People of all religious and cultural backgrounds are welcome to attend.

Recreational marijuana has been legal in Colorado since 2008, and Denver became the first city in the United States to decriminalize possession of psilocybin mushrooms in 2019. So who's to judge a few stoners who celebrate marijuana as a holy sacrament in a 100-year-old building? The debates you had with your college roommate about the epistemological nature of God now have an official home.

This building retains the stately, ivy-covered belfry and beautiful stained-glass windows from its days as a Lutheran church, but today's services include laser light shows and guided meditations. The interior walls are painted in miraculously trippy murals that are certainly augmented by the euphoria and hallucinogenic properties associated with marijuana. Refreshingly, Elevationists claim no divine authority and eschew authoritarian structures. The congregation claims to value each person's spiritual journey and believes the marijuana plant can "accelerate" this personal quest for meaning. Don't worry, this is not a cult.

Address 400 S Logan Street, Denver, CO 80209, +1 (303) 800-5644, www.elevationists.org | Getting there Bus 3 to Alameda Avenue & S Pearl Street | Hours Fri–Mon noon–8pm, Tue–Thu 4–8pm | Tip The Church nightclub is housed in a former Episcopal church from 1889 with spectacular vaulted ceilings. Today's worship is sweaty, late-night dancing to thumping DJ music (1160 Lincoln Street, www.coclubs.com).

55 King Baptist Church
Earth, Wind & Fire but no brimstone

You don't have to be Christian to feel the rhapsodic power of gospel music. One of six Baptist Churches clustered around Martin Luther King Jr. Boulevard east of downtown, this King Baptist Church was named in honor of Dr. King himself. It's been a beacon for Denver's Black community for more than 50 years.

The Sunday church services here are a musical celebration, and visitors are welcome. The congregation's Mass Choir sings rapturous gospel hymns and has even recorded an album with Denver son and former choir boy Philip Bailey, future lead singer, arranger, and percussionist for legendary funk band Earth, Wind & Fire. Feel the love and raise your voice with the gospel chorus at King Baptist.

Philip Bailey graduated from East High School then attended Metropolitan State and University of Colorado before being invited to join Earth, Wind & Fire, which dominated FM radio in the 1970s and 1980s. Bailey and his bandmates have released 22 albums to date (including tracks recorded at Caribou Ranch recording studio in Nederland), and their music has been covered or sampled by everyone from Whitney Houston and Taylor Swift to Jay-Z and Public Enemy. The band is one of the all-time great and top-selling R&B / funk acts, redefining the entire genre of Afro pop by taking inspiration from gospel and soul music. The band was inducted in the Rock & Roll Hall of Fame in 2000, and Bailey was inducted into the Colorado Music Hall of Fame in 2017 (see ch. 95).

A local hero, Bailey is a masterful percussionist, but it's his four-octave voice that's kept him onstage and performing for the last five decades. His vocal instrument can soar in falsetto or plunge to bass, skipping about with syncopated brilliance. He's also an insightful songwriter and arranger, admittedly influenced by Stevie Wonder and jazz. Bailey scored his biggest solo hit "Easy Lover" with Phil Collins in 1984.

Address 3370 Ivy Street, Denver, CO 80207, +1 (303) 388-3248, www.kingbaptist.org |
Getting there Bus 34 to 35th Avenue & Holly Street | Hours Services and bible study
daily, check website for times | Tip Across the street from King Baptist, Skyland Park is
an indulgent swath of greenery. Walk the dog, or chill in the shade, as kids romp on the
playground (5600 E 35th Avenue).

56 La Alma-Lincoln Park

Stroll through the city's newest cultural district

The City of Denver finally recognized Westside's La Alma Lincoln Park neighborhood as a Historic Cultural District in 2021, joining Five Points as one of Denver's only two cultural districts. This designation was a major win for the city's Hispanic community, which has long contributed to the city's cultural and economic vibrancy. The Hispanic community makes up more than 30 percent of the city's entire population and strongly informs Denver's identity. Mexican pride is alive here as well. Denver hosts one of the country's largest *Cinco de Mayo* festivals, and, come November, the sugar skulls of *Día de los Muertos* are everywhere.

The La Alma Lincoln Park neighborhood is a great place to go for a stroll. It was originally built for railroad workers, starting in the 1880s, and around half the neighborhood was constructed by 1905. Look for the brightly painted brick homes that are the architectural signature here. Comfortably residential, it's also peppered with small stucco-sided homes, and the active street life is apparent when you walk about. Neighbors here are happy to stop for a chat with you. Everyone here truly rallied to petition the city to become a Historic Cultural District.

La Alma Park itself was once the site of Cheyenne and Arapaho Native American encampments. The geometric mural by Emanuel Martinez on the outer wall of the park's La Alma Recreation Center was painted in 1978. The center remains a point of local pride and was a gathering spot for Chicano Movement protests in the 1960s and 1970s, as several important leaders of the Chicano Movement lived here. The mural depicts the multilayered experience of Latino identity by interweaving indigenous iconography with modern symbols. Cherished education pioneer Emily Griffith, who founded the eponymous technical college across from the park in 1916, lived in the neighborhood, too.

Address La Alma Recreation Center, 1325 W 11th Avenue, Denver, CO 80204, www.historicdenver.org/la-alma | Getting there Bus 1, 9 to Klamath Street & W 13th Avenue | Hours Unrestricted | Tip The distinctive pink walls of Museo de las Americas (861 Santa Fe Drive, www.museo.org) hint at the creativity within. The Chicano Humanities and Arts Council (www.chacgallery.org) was founded in 1978 and hosts visual and performing arts events and gallery shows.

57 Lakeside Amusement Park
Park of the people

For almost 60 years, the premier attraction at Lakeside Amusement Park was Lakeside Speedway, a short-track auto raceway. Loud and dangerous action entertained fans here until 1988, when a racecar lost control and careened into the stands, killing a bystander, maiming a young girl, and injuring several others. This grisly accident prompted the track to shut down almost immediately. It's been permanently mothballed and rotting in place ever since. Visitors can still spy the speedway's crumbling façade over a fence at the south end of the park or from the top of the Zoom Tower ride.

Once promoted as "Paris on the Platte," Denver had early ambitions to be more than just an overgrown mining-supply depot. In this spirit, the owners of Lakeside Amusement Park originally named it White City, a naked ploy to associate itself with the magnificent World's Fair in Chicago. Opened in 1908, the Park boasted lovely gardens designed by Frederick Law Olmsted, the landscape architect who designed Central Park in New York City.

The Lakeside Amusement Park founders also went so far as to create the entirely new municipality of Lakeside in order to avoid Denver's rules prohibiting the sale of alcohol. The park was a raucous attraction with dancehalls, bars, theaters, and a swimming pool. Many of the original buildings and attractions remain in operation, including the antiquarian hand-carved carousel and miniature train. The Cyclone, an infamous wooden roller coaster, has tousled children's hair for generations.

There's not a nicer place in Denver to stroll on a warm summer night and people watch. Sunset over the mountains is made more beautiful by the reflections in Lake Rhoda. With Elitch Gardens & Water Park slated to move from downtown out towards the airport, Lakeside will carry the torch of Denver's unintentionally retro (aka old), wholesome family entertainment.

Address 4601 Sheridan Boulevard, Denver, CO 80212, +1 (303) 477-1621, www.lakesideamusementpark.com | Getting there Bus 44, 51 to W 44th Avenue & Sheridan Boulevard | Hours May–Sep, Mon–Fri 6–11pm, Sat & Sun noon–11pm | Tip Water World is a far more kinetic (and wet) experience. With 34 attractions, this is obligatory summer fun (8801 North Pecos Street, Federal Heights, www.waterworldcolorado.com).

58 Learned Lemur
It's ok to like creepy stuff

Jonathan Alberico has been fascinated by the morbidly beautiful since he was a kid. He grew up rummaging about in his parents' antique shop on South Broadway, and he's taken his passion for old things a step further – and darker – at the Learned Lemur.

This curio shop carries on the lost tradition of Victorian-era curiosity rooms by showcasing scientific knowledge and arcane instruments for emotional impact. No skeletons in the closet here; they're the main attraction. There's even a complete female human skeleton (sans skull) from the 1920s, with her original rib cage cartilage still intact, black and ossified. As Aspenite (ok, Woody Creeker) Hunter S. Thompson liked to say, "When the going gets weird, the weird turn pro."

The permanence of bones is terrifyingly beautiful. Mute totems of the hidden workings of life itself, bones outlast us by far. Learned Lemur employs flesh-eating beetles to clean the carcasses of animals large and small to produce the white animal skeletons on display. The work of artist team Rocky Mountain Punk is also displayed here with meticulous dioramas of flowers, butterflies, and animal skulls.

Alberico's collection stimulates our compulsive attraction to death. His interests span from old medical devices and apothecary bottles to taxidermy and driftwood. Where else can you study 19th-century leather cases filled with eyeglass lenses or gawk at the mounted, nine-foot-tall bust of an actual giraffe? Alberico worked at the Wizard's Chest for years (see ch. 111) and has a flair for the theatrical. The second level of his 1896 brick building is shared with a tattoo parlor, and the enclosed performance space in the back courtyard (shared with Bruz Off Fax brewery) is accessed via a secret door behind a bookcase. Sword swallowers, snake charmers, and burlesque dancers perform here in boisterous reviews.

Address 2220 E Colfax Avenue, Denver, CO 80206, +1 (720) 600-7585, www.learnedlemur.com | Getting there Bus 24 to York Street & Colfax Avenue | Hours Mon–Sat 11am–7pm, Sun noon–5pm | Tip Denver Museum of Miniatures, Dolls, and Toys showcases the strange world of antique miniatures. Think: Japanese dolls, mini planes and trains, and fully-furnished dollhouses (830 Kipling Street, Lakewood, www.dmmdt.org).

59_Little Caesar's Last Stand
Where Joe Roma was murdered in cold blood

Italian immigrants were among Colorado's early European settlers during the Pikes Peak Gold Rush of 1859. Many emigrated from Potenza in southern Italy, where racketeering and extortion had been formalized by La Cosa Nostra, aka the mafia. Some of these *paisanos* brought their Old World traditions with them and used Prohibition in their favor, running liquor up and down the Front Range. There were approximately 30 gang-related murders in Colorado between 1919 and 1933. Chicago mobster Al Capone was known to park his bullet-proof Cadillac in front of Patsy's Italian restaurant when he cavorted in Colorado.

One of Denver's original kingpins was Joe Roma, aka Little Caesar. Roma stood just 5'1", but he was a giant of bootlegging and, as such, had competitors. He split the local rackets with various frenemies and was implicated in turf-related gang wars. Roma was as ruthless and conniving as he was loved and respected in the community. He paid off neighbors to be his eyes and ears on the street, and he allegedly bribed police and politicians too. It was also common knowledge that he killed when necessary, dumping one victim on a remote dirt road near Pueblo to send a message to his challengers.

Roma's luck ran out on February 18, 1933, when he was shot dead, assassination-style, at this very house, just around the corner from Our Lady of Mount Carmel Catholic Church (see ch. 75). His wife found him slumped in his favorite chair after a business meeting. Interestingly, the Smaldone family (Roma's chief rivals) prospered wildly after taking over Roma's bootlegging and gambling operations.

An iron-fisted crime syndicate, the Smaldone family amassed local power and influence. Leader Clyde Smaldone met both Herbert Hoover and Franklin D. Roosevelt. The family even developed the gambling industry in Central City, effectively running the town in the 1940s.

Address 3504 Vallejo Street, Denver, CO 80211 | **Getting there** Bus 44 to Tejon Street & 36th Avenue | **Hours** Unrestricted | **Tip** The building that houses Tamales by La Casita was once the Alpine Inn and owned by former University of Colorado football star John "Skip" LaGuardia. A mafia enforcer, LaGuardia was shot and bludgeoned to death in 1973 (3561 Tejon Street).

60 Little Raven Street
Short street with a long memory

Little Raven Street borders languorous Commons Park along the South Platte River. Less than a mile long, it honors Chief Hosa (c.1810–1889), aka Little Raven, a leader of the Southern Arapaho, who notably welcomed white goldminers when the area was settled in 1858. As you walk down this street, remember that local Native Americans from several tribes still live and thrive in the Front Range, including Utes, Cheyenne, Comanche, and Apache.

There's a modest nationwide push to reconcile the genocide inflicted on Native Americans, who experience disproportionate violence, poverty, and substance abuse, but Denver has a ways to go. Downtown's Wazee and Wewatta Streets are named for the Native American wives of mountain man William W. McGaa (1824–1867), a swindler whose land dealings helped establish Denver itself.

Little Raven was a respected negotiator and peacemaker. He brokered peace between native tribes and did his best to secure favorable treaties with the US government – all of which were broken. After the horrific Sand Creek massacre in southeastern Colorado in 1864, which left at least 150 of his people dead, Little Raven redoubled his efforts and successfully negotiated the tribe's modern-day reservation in Oklahoma.

The athletic ability and kinetic artistry of the skaters at Denver Skatepark, at the corner of Little Raven and 20th Streets, would likely have impressed the young Arapaho warriors who grew up on this very spot by the South Platte River. The Arapaho hunted buffalo here and cultivated a powerful warrior culture. They also loved to gamble and play games, including lacrosse, which was invented by the Iroquois. In an odd full circle, the University of Denver is a perennial contender in Division 1 NCAA Men's Lacrosse and won the national championship in 2015. A lacrosse team representing the Iroquois Nation will compete at the World Games in 2022.

Address Little Raven Street, Denver, CO 80202, www.denver.org/listing/commons-park |
Getting there Bus 19 to 20th & Little Raven Streets; RTD Rail to Union Station
(E, W Lines) | Hours Unrestricted | Tip Sand Creek National Historic site is a chilling
memorial to the reality of genocidal violence against Native Americans, which continues to
this day (55411 County Road W, Eads, www.nps.gov/sand/index.htm).

61 Lucky Bikes Re-Cyclery

A community hub with spokes

The name and circular logo of this bike shop are reminiscent of Lucky Strike cigarette branding, which is appropriate somehow. Denver is a working-class, blue-collar town at heart, and life on Federal Avenue is not the most glamorous. This is the kind neighborhood where a community-centered, social enterprise bike shop is right at home next to a decrepit, octagonal-shaped liquor store and the dual-purpose hair salon/insurance agency down the street.

The founders of this non-profit enterprise have been at it since 2013, and their halos shine bright. In addition to being a full-service bike shop staffed by experienced professionals who can do any repair or upgrade, Lucky Bikes Re-Cyclery is 100 percent committed to community enrichment via the joys, health benefits, and economic efficiency of cycling, not to mention its low impact on the environment. They recycle used bicycles and sell them at affordable prices. And they teach bicycle maintenance through a well-established volunteer program. When you donate an old or unused bike, you can rest assured that it will see new life with someone who really needs it. The large fleet of mismatched bikes out front is a welcome sight.

The team here runs Lucky to Ride, a non-profit program for youth ages 8–20. This group of committed cyclists, educators, and community leaders takes underserved and at-risk kids into nature for mountain biking adventures. They offer a series of programs for empowering youth, as well as volunteer opportunities. Kids can work towards earning a bicycle through volunteer hours in the shop.

Colorado truly is cycling crazy, with its history of big races and rides (Red Zinger Bicycle Classic, Triple Bypass, etc.) and goofy cycling culture (Denver Cruiser Ride). Lucky Bikes Re-Cyclery and Lucky to Ride contribute enormously to the city's biking community by creating new generations of enthusiasts.

Address 3150 W Jewell Avenue, Denver, CO 80219, +1 (720) 454-9722, www.luckybikes.org | Getting there Bus 30, 31 to S Federal Boulevard & W Jewel Avenue | Hours Tue–Fri 11am–6pm, Sat 10am–5pm | Tip Randy's Recycled Cycles is another great, community-focused bike store and repair shop specializing in refurbishing and selling used bikes (2301 Champa Street, www.randysrecycledcycles.com).

62 Mayan Theater
Movie magic with architectural flair

This art deco masterpiece from 1930 makes you long for the days when people actually dressed up to go out in public. The building is elegant, charming, and campy all at once. The doors opened here when streetcars still ran up and down Broadway, so ditch your sweatpants and hoody and try to look sharp for shows at the Mayan.

"Art Deco Mayan Revival" is an actual architectural style from the 1920s and 1930s that drew inspiration from pre-Columbian Mesoamerican iconography and architectural cues. Clearly, the distinctive face and headdress that top the building are not typical of Denver. Now a historic landmark, the Mayan has a big main auditorium, plus two smaller theaters where the balcony used to be. It's an "arthouse" theater that mainly shows independent and foreign films, documentaries, concert films, similar to the Sie Film Center on Colfax Avenue and the newly remodeled Esquire Theatre. The entire building can be rented out for events.

There's a full bar upstairs, so getting here early before the show to discuss art with your cultured friends is a premium. You can get a proper espresso too and real butter drizzled on the fresh popcorn. The main screen has a thick, classic curtain, and the plush, retro chairs are comfortable if a bit cramped. The theater may be run by behemoth Landmark Theaters, but the street-side ticket booth makes coming here feel special.

The Mayan was slated for demolition in 1984, but Denverites formed an organization called Friends of the Mayan, which helped save the theater and organized its restoration. (The development company of former Broncos owner Pat Bowlen came to the rescue and purchased the entire block.) Colorful murals and distinctive stonework decorate the interior, and the informative displays on the building's restoration are pleasingly educational. An evening here is an event – and the perfect first date.

Address 110 Broadway, Denver, CO 80203, +1 (303) 744-6799, www.landmarktheatres.com/denver/mayan-theatre/info | **Getting there** Bus 0, 0L to Broadway & W 1st Avenue | **Hours** See website for showtimes | **Tip** Summer evenings at 88 Drive-In Theater offer a quaint reminder that Denver has not outgrown itself (8780 Rosemary Street, Commerce City, www.denvermartdrivein.com).

63__Meow Wolf

The art collective goes intergalactic

No spoilers, but *Convergence Station,* Meow Wolf's Denver installation, draws inspiration from the Americans with Disabilities
Act (ADA) from 1978. This pioneering legislation was brought to
national attention by the Denver-based Gang of 19, heroic activists
in wheelchairs who demanded to "boldly go where everyone has
gone before." They blocked city buses to highlight unequal access to
public transportation. The interdimensional galaxies of *Convergence
Station,* an intergalactic transfer hub run by the "Quantum Department of Transportation," are discovered by a certain bus-driving
adventurer.

Proudly maximalist, Meow Wolf is nothing if not high concept, a good match for industrial and innovative Denver. After all,
the city attracts visionary businesses like Boom Supersonic, which
is determined to reintroduce sound-breaking commercial jets like
the Concorde. The new darlings of "immersive, nonlinear themed
entertainment," Meow Wolf is a collective of genre-bending merry
pranksters originally from Santa Fe, New Mexico, that has basically
invented a new medium: transforming entire buildings into fungible
art experiences. *Convergence Station* is the group's third permanent
installation, after Santa Fe and Las Vegas, and the most ambitious
yet at 94,000 square feet and spanning four floors.

The project took five years to conceive and build, and the result is
spectacular. Located next to Mile High Stadium and tucked under
crisscrossing freeway overpasses, the rounded, smooth building is
on the site of a former steel factory. The exhibit even incorporates a
1940s Coors delivery truck found on location. More than 110 artists from Denver collaborated with about 150 Meow Wolf artists to
create the space. The inmates are most definitely in charge of this
bedazzled asylum, "a social-impact art project that fuels business, and
a business that fuels social-impact art projects."

Address 1338 1st Street, Denver, CO 80204, +1 (720) 729-1200, www.meowwolf.com | Getting there Bus 15L to Decatur Street & Federal Boulevard; RTD Rail to Empower Field at Mile High Station (C, E, W Lines) | Hours Sun–Thu 10am–10pm, Fri & Sat 10am–midnight | Tip RedLine Contemporary Art Center is committed to art as positive social change. There's an excellent gallery and suite of events and programs here (2350 Arapahoe Avenue, www.redlineart.org).

64 Mile High Comics

Emporium of pop culture ephemera

Several 30-foot-tall reproductions of iconic comic book covers drape the side of this building, proudly blaring the store's national significance on the collecting scene. Mile High Comics claims to be the largest store of its kind in the country. Owner Chuck Rozanski has been buying, selling, trading, and collecting comic books since 1969, when he started the business in his parents' basement. His industrial-zoned warehouse is a testament to a dream realized: promoting comics as an artform.

The sheer volume of collectible pop culture here is beyond counting. Mile High Comics is less a "store" than it is the gravitational center of a certain kind of universe – a black hole of childhood nostalgia. Two-thirds of this mega-warehouse are given over to dark, dusty storage areas for the company's robust online sales. The remaining third is a maddening clutter of magazines, comic books, figurines, stuffed animals, toys, magnets, and much more.

Trading cards are not the specialty of Rozanski and his staff, but a signed, special edition of basketball player Lebron James' rookie trading card is valued at $5 million. People take the collecting of printed paper very seriously, in other words. Rare comics books have sold for more than $3 million dollars, and there are comics on display here for $3,000 and more. But you can also buy "mystery boxes" of comic books priced by the pound. And there are sagging tables of $1 comics, too. The flow of incoming and outgoing inventory is constant, so you'll want to make a habit of stopping by regularly.

Looking for Monty Python figurines of characters from *The Holy Grail?* Mile High Comics has you covered: $125 each. The store hosts regular gaming tournaments, and role-playing games are well represented. There are sections devoted to *Star Wars* and *Star Trek*, of course. Rozanski also has a large collection of Native American pottery that's "still being curated."

Address 4600 Jason Street, Denver, CO 80211, +1 (303) 477-0042, www.milehighcomics.com | Getting there Bus 19, 52 to Lipan Street & W 46th Avenue | Hours Mon–Fri 9am–6pm, Sat 10am–6pm, Sun 11am–5pm | Tip Fifty-two 80's sells toys and memorabilia from the 1980s. Even their pixelated, Atari-like website is a goofy throwback to an era when Saturday morning cartoons were still a thing (1874 S Broadway, www.the80sareawesome.com).

65 Mile-High Marker
Step up to the Colorado State Capitol

The brass plaque on the 13th step leading up to the magnificent Colorado State Capitol spells it out: *5,280 feet* – exactly one English statute mile above sea level.

The city's first mile-high marker plaque was placed on these stone steps in 1909, although it was placed on the 15th step and repeatedly stolen. It was relocated twice over the decades for accuracy, making for an odd total of two brass markers and one stone engraving on three different steps. In 2003, land surveyors determined that the 13th step was the best spot for it. Still, despite the marker's short but eventful journey to the 13th step, a moniker was born! Today, the Mile High City flexes this unique cred with plaques and informal markers throughout the city and a staggering number of local businesses that incorporate "mile high" into their name.

The gold leaf dome of the Colorado State Capitol is certainly more recognizable, but the combination indoors of white marble floors (sourced in Marble, Colorado) and rose onyx wainscoting (aka Beulah marble, sourced near Pueblo) is enthralling. The effect instills a certain pride knowing that stone like this was geologically formed in Colorado and quarried and polished here by local talent. Match this luster to the building's shiny brass railings and hardwood door trims, and you almost have to wear sunglasses indoors.

It's worth noting the capital of New Mexico in Santa Fe is quite a bit higher at 7,199 feet, but that building has not been awarded LEED Gold certification. The colossal bulk of our building is recognized for environmental design because it's kept warm and cooled by geothermal power sourced from wells more than 350 feet underground. This technology nearly eliminates the need for burning fossil fuels and has saved taxpayers millions of dollars. Heating coal was originally brought in on subterranean railcars, but these tunnels have since been expanded to connect nearby government buildings.

ONE MILE ABOVE SEA LEVEL

Address 200 E Colfax Avenue, Denver, CO 80203, www.capitol.colorado.gov | Getting there Bus 0L, 3L, 8, 19 to Civic Center | Hours See website for free tours Mon–Sat | Tip Why is there a single row of purple seats that rings the upper deck of Coors Field? These 865 odd-colored seats mark exactly 5,280 feet above sea level and span the 300 section of this Major League Baseball stadium horizontally (2001 Blake Street, www.mlb.com/rockies).

66 Millennium Bridge
Steel-rigged masts are a city theme

Look down the 16th Street Mall from the northwest corner of the Colorado State Capitol (see ch. 65), and you can see Millennium Bridge framed by the sandstone Flatirons and Longs Peak (14,259 feet high). Walk down Brown's Bluff, and enjoy LoDo and Larimer Square before coming to the train tracks. Then walk up and over Millennium Bridge and the huffing trains hauling coal to amble through Confluence Park and over Platte River Bridge. Keep going to cross Highland Bridge, which spans I-25. These three pedestrian-only bridges link the hills that form Denver's casual downtown – an outdoorsy mix of industrial, riparian, and artistic.

Intentionally or not, an architectural theme of white tubes of steel runs through all three bridges. The look is almost identical to the masts and cables that hold up the iconic roof of Denver International Airport. These soaring, white canopies, which instantly evoke a snow-capped mountain range, predate the bridges by years and were erected in 1995 by steel fabricator Zimmerman Metals, whose red cursive neon sign is familiar to any I-25 driver. The system of masts and cables that keep the canopies afloat were originally a cost-saving design that has become a city-wide theme.

Architecturally bold and seemingly out of place, the Millennium Bridge was completed in 2002 and looks exactly like the mast of a ship. It lacks the airport's canopies, but the bridge's singular, 200-foot-tall mast of tubular steel is painted brilliant white. It weighs 110 tons and acts as a "compression strut" for the support cables anchored to the cement foundation.

A courtly plaza with benches and public art hovers 35 feet over the railroad tracks below. It's hard not to be reminded of the Conestoga wagons, or "prairie schooners," that transported European settlers across the Great Plains to Denver. Their white canopies looked like little ships sailing across the tall grasses.

Address West-End Terminus of the 16th Street Mall, Denver, CO 80202, www.denver.org |
Getting there Bus Mall Ride to Millennium Bridge; RTD Rail to Union Station (C, E,
R, W Lines) | Hours Unrestricted | Tip Early real estate developers marketed Denver as
"Paris on the Platte", a shill that's finally come true. When crossing the Platte River Bridge
(between South Platte River Trail and Commons Park, Denver), look for the "locks of love,"
a tradition adopted from Pont des Arts bridge over the Seine River in Paris, where lovers
attach padlocks as symbols of their unbreakable bond.

67 Molly Brown Museum
The most-famous Titanic *survivor*

Margaret Brown was aboard the RMS *Titanic* returning from Paris in 1914 to attend to a sick grandchild when the ship struck the infamous iceberg. She rowed her lifeboat and argued with a crew member who refused to turn back and help rescue more people. Brown demonstrated pluck like this throughout her life, but her catchy nickname "The Unsinkable Molly Brown" was conferred by the *Rocky Mountain News* only after she died.

A wealthy mining heiress, Brown was better known in life for being a suffragist and philanthropist. She ran for the US Senate in 1914 to represent Colorado in a longshot bid to earn women the right to vote. After the Ludlow Massacre of striking miners in southern Colorado, she helped broker a deal between the Rockefeller conglomerate and labor interests. She was awarded the French Legion of Honor for her volunteerism in World War I and was a founding member of the Denver chapter of Alliance Française (see ch. 7).

Her home is now an immaculately preserved museum on Pennsylvania Avenue in the Capitol Hill neighborhood. Completed in 1889, the building did not suit Brown's theatrical extravagance. She insisted on adding a massive stone staircase, flanked by lion statues and strangely sexualized sphinxes, to make it look more impressive from the street. Also note the old flagstone pillar on the sidewalk out front for hitching horses, one of many around Capitol Hill.

Among other improvements, Brown and her husband, who owned a goldmine in Leadville, also replaced the roof with tiles imported from France. Designed by architect William Lang, who drew about 300 buildings around Denver, the building is constructed of rhyolite and sandstone quarried in Castle Rock and the Garden of the Gods, respectively. Look for the stained-glass window by the grand staircase, a swirl of mesmerizing patterns and recently restored as part of a $2-million renovation.

Address 1340 Pennsylvania Street, Denver, CO 80203, +1 (303) 832-4092, www.mollybrown.org | Getting there Bus 10 to 12th Avenue & Pennsylvania Street | Hours Tue–Sun 10am–4pm | Tip Housed in an exquisite brick mansion from 1883, the Center for Colorado Women's History pays extra attention to the stalwart women who helped their sisters finally earn the vote in national elections in 1920 (1310 Bannock Street, www.historycolorado.org).

68__Mork & Mindy's House
The spirit of "Nanu Nanu" lives on

This beautiful Victorian built in 1900 is the location for the beloved television sitcom *Mork & Mindy* (1978–1982). The show introduced the world to former street mime and standup comedian Robin Williams, who improvised much of the dialogue before a live studio audience in California. Playing Mork in rainbow suspenders was Williams' big break, catapulting him into movies and global stardom. The show also cemented Boulder in public consciousness as a fun, free-wheeling place. Mindy let Mork live in the attic, until they became lovers in later episodes and birthed hilarious Johnathan Winters. (Stephen King's *The Stand* is also set in Boulder.)

The show's creators chose Boulder, sometimes called Berkeley of the Rockies, for its reputation as an alternative, open-minded community. Pam Dawber's character Mindy McConnell attended the University of Colorado, a strong influence on town culture since 1876. You wouldn't expect a 21-year-old college student to live in a 3,818 square foot, seven-bedroom house, but that's Boulder. This town is chockablock with fortunate students who like to party in stately 19th-century rentals. Victorian architecture is a Boulder signature thanks to the early mining wealth. Walk around the Whittier neighborhood from this house to see some beautiful examples.

Mork & Mindy was surprisingly accurate in other ways too. Mindy drove a ragtop Jeep Wrangler, now the unofficial car of CU students. The show's opening and closing credits featured shots of the iconic Flatirons rock formations, Chautauqua Park, Pearl Street, and CU's Folsom Field stadium.

Since Robin William's tragic suicide in 2014, this house has become a touchstone for his fans. (So has the Williams mural on E 13th Avenue and Grant Street in Denver, which honors him as Mork.) However this building is an actual home, and there is no public access. Please be respectful.

Address 1619 Pine Street, Boulder, CO 80302 | Getting there Bus FF 1 to Downtown Boulder Station | Hours Unrestricted from the outside only | Tip Designed by architect Charles Deaton, the futuristic, bulbous "Sleeper House" was featured in Woody Allen's movie *Sleeper* (1973). The "Orgasmatron" is, in fact, the building's circular elevator (855 Visionary Trail, Golden).

69 Mount Evans Scenic Byway

Drive up Denver's summit views

To drive up 14,256-foot Mount Evans is a local rite of passage. This is Denver's backyard, after all. The area is part of Denver's Mountain Parks and includes the noble Echo Lake Lodge, a log-masterpiece constructed in 1926. Hiking up mountain peaks is the unofficial Colorado pastime. Not everyone has the physique or skillset to hike or rock climb, though, which makes Mount Evans Scenic Byway a windshield hiker's dream. Welcome to the highest-elevation paved road in America! (Note that it's only open from Memorial Day to late summer/early fall, weather permitting.)

You can drive up Pikes Peak as well, but Mount Evans feels wilder. There's a grove of protected bristlecone pine trees on the way up, some of which have been dated to more than 2,500 years old. There's no cog railroad or restaurant, but plenty of goats and marmots.

There is, however, a stone ruin at the summit of Mount Evans that looks like an organic outgrowth of the mountain itself. A former restaurant called Crest House, this "castle in the sky" was built by a romantic German immigrant to impress his fiancée. The futuristic building was meant to resemble a shooting star and was designed by Colorado architect Edwin A. Francis. A fire destroyed much of the structure in 1979, but a gnarl of soaring timbers and industrial steel stands to this day. Financially troublesome to construct, staff, and maintain, it was never rebuilt.

With eight major mountain ranges and a total of 56 mountains 14,000 feet tall or higher, Colorado has the highest average elevation of all 50 states, at 6,860.6 feet. Three of these so-called "14ers" are clearly visible from downtown: Mount Evans, Longs Peak (14,259'), and Pikes Peak (14,115'). These white-topped giants punctuate the Rocky Mountain vistas to the West.

Address Mount Evans Scenic Byway, Evergreen, CO 80439, +1 (303) 567-4382, www.codot.gov/travel/colorado-byways/north-central/mount-evans | Getting there By car, from I-70, take Exit 240 in Idaho Springs, then south on Route 5 | Hours Unrestricted Memorial Day–Labor Day | Tip The Pikes Peak Highway west of Colorado Springs takes you to the mountain's 14,115-foot summit. The annual Pikes Peak International Hill Climb auto race is highly competitive (5089 Pikes Peak Highway, Cascade).

70___My Brother's Bar
Skid row never felt so at home

The original, 20-foot scroll of Jack Kerouac's generation-defining book *On the Road* may be housed in the American Writers Museum in Chicago, but the incandescent spirit of inspiration for the story is still alive in Denver's old gin joints. The book's protagonist Neal Cassady was born and raised in Denver, spending "a third of his time in the pool hall, a third in jail, and a third in the public library," according to Kerouac.

Originally founded three years before Colorado earned statehood, My Brother's Bar is a looking glass back into Denver's grubby, Victorian days. Cowboys, miners, and merchants trying to make good at the edge of American civilization in 1873 drank a lot of booze. By the 1950s, parts of Denver were skid rows with derelict residence hotels and seedy bars. Neal Cassady's father was a down-and-out wino, and young Cassady was left to roam free. This freedom included running up a bar tab at My Brother's Bar. When teenage Cassady was shipped off to reform school in Buena Vista, Colorado, for compulsively stealing cars, he wrote a letter to a friend asking him to pay his tab. The framed original hangs on the wall to this day.

The drunken revelry of the state's early days prompted the Colorado legislature to amend the Colorado Tavern License and require establishments serving alcohol to sell prepared food. Food helps mitigate the effects of alcohol somewhat, and Denver bars vary in their commitment to fine cuisine. My Brother's Bar keeps it simple, but customers are rewarded with the kitchen's passionate devotion to all-American burgers, beef or bison.

Beat Generation poet Allen Ginsburg also lived and worked in Denver for a time and was friends with Cassady and Kerouac. He was a known patron here and penned rambling odes to the city. Ginsburg later helped found Buddhist-inspired Naropa University in Boulder (see ch. 6).

Address 2376 15th Street, Denver, CO 80202, +1 (303) 455-9991, www.mybrothersbar.com |
Getting there Bus 28, 32, 44 to 15th & Platte Streets | Hours Fri & Sat 11am–11pm,
Mon–Thu 11am–10pm | Tip Denver's best neighborhood bar, The Thin Man shares
outdoor seating (and ownership) with St. Mark's Coffeehouse. A dependable cast of
characters comes here to stay up late and drink house-infused vodkas and fine coffees
(2015 E 17th Avenue).

71 National Ballpark Museum

America's pastime, brick by brick

Your chance to see the legendary Ebbets Field ended with its demolition in 1960. The home field of the Brooklyn Dodgers was constructed in 1913 and was one of the so-called "jewel box" stadiums of Major League Baseball, wood and steel edifices that made the game feel intimate compared to today's cement megastructures. Visit the National Ballpark Museum, however, and you'll see original light fixtures from the Ebbets Field entry rotunda.

Wonderful obscura like this are what make a visit here so satisfying. Who knew reading the line items of Babe Ruth's hefty tax return would be so irresistible? Baseball stops time somehow, allowing fans to measure their lives against its steady presence. America's pastime is "only" a game, but it's also a place. Beyond the infield diamond, the dimensions of the outfield are unique to every ballpark and create a unique experience of play. This museum cherishes baseball's magical places, like a newspaper clipping describing the last game ever played in the original Tiger Stadium in Detroit. In the bottom of the 8th inning, Tiger Robert Fick hit the final home run in the last game ever played there – a game-winning grand slam and the 11,111th home run ever hit in that park.

Local Negro League teams played at Sonny Lawson Park, near the Blair-Caldwell African American Research Library (see. ch. 15) in Five Points, where a melancholy Jack Kerouac describes seeing multi-ethnic players "performing with heart-breaking seriousness" in *On the Road*.

The museum's building is historic in its own right, a classic brick and timber warehouse from 1895. The Denver Bears (later the Denver Zephyrs), the local minor league team founded in 1885 that fed players to the Yankees and Cardinals, fittingly get their very own gallery. Opened in 1948, Bears Stadium regularly drew crowds of 20,000 or more and stood just west of downtown, where the Mile High Stadium complex sprawls today.

Address 1940 Blake Street, Denver, CO 80202, +1 (303) 974-5835, www.ballparkmuseum.com | Getting there Bus 52 to 20th & Blake Streets; RTD Rail to Union Station (C, E, R, W Lines) | Hours See website | Tip The Museum of Contemporary Art, just a 10-minute walk down the street, bursts with originality (1485 Delgany Street, www.mcadenver.org).

72 NOAA Boulder
Yes, science is real

In 1807, President Thomas Jefferson led the formation of the nation's original science agency, the National Geologic Survey, which eventually morphed into the National Oceanic & Atmospheric Administration (NOAA). This federal agency is based in Washington, DC, but its Boulder facility is critical to the agency's mission: "To understand and predict changes in climate, weather, oceans, and coasts, to share that knowledge and information with others, and to conserve and manage coastal and marine ecosystems and resources."

Visitors can tour the Boulder facility and see aspects of the four Earth Systems Laboratories (Chemical Sciences, Global Monitoring, Global Systems, and Physical Sciences), National Centers for Environmental Information, and the regional National Weather Service. Research by scientists here penetrates the sun, the deepest oceans, and all the weather systems on Earth.

With more than 12,000 employees and an annual budget of $5.35 billion, NOAA generates volumes of research that informs policy ranging from fisheries and hurricane responses to aviation and navigation systems. America's "environmental intelligence agency" maintains a fleet of satellites, and data produced by NOAA is said to help propel 1/3 of the country's gross domestic product (GDP).

Once considered "scientific Siberia" by the research community, Boulder has proved advantageous for its geologic stability and geographic isolation. The NOAA tours take you deep into weather prediction, satellite technology, solar-terrestrial physics and more. The Science on a Sphere display uses a sophisticated computer and projector system to explain atmospheric storms, climate change, and ocean currents. You also learn how solar flares and other extra-planetary forces affect Earth. And global warming comes into sharp focus after spending time at the Carbon Cycle Greenhouse Gasses display.

Address 325 Broadway, Boulder, CO 80305, +1 (303) 497-4000, www.boulder.noaa.gov | Getting there Bus DASH and SKIP to Broadway & Rayleigh Road | Hours Call for tour information | Tip The slab-like National Center for Atmospheric Research looms on a hill in south Boulder and offers tours too. It was designed by architect I. M. Pei, whose most famous work is the pyramidal glass entrance to the Louvre museum in Paris (1850 Table Mesa Drive, Boulder, www.scied.ucar.edu).

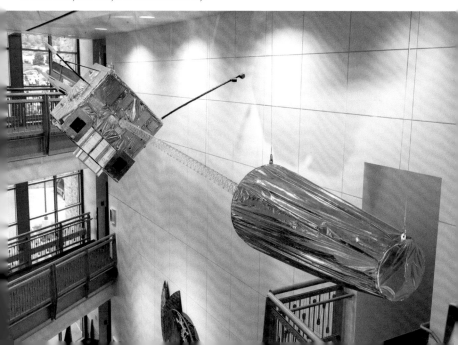

73 __Novo Coffee
Denver's best coffee

Founded in 2002 by a local family of Denverites, this place is heaven on Earth for coffee snobs. You know a coffee shop means business when it buys a hand-built MVP Hydra espresso machine from Synesso in Seattle. Heavy as a stack of lead ingots, complicated as a nuclear submarine, and selling for around $20,000 at the top end, Synesso espresso machines are known for operating at precise, stable temperatures and even pressure. This superior mechanical engineering ensures the creamy, rich flavor that espresso "pulls" are known for and that coffee lovers dream of.

Perhaps more importantly, Novo air-roasts their own beans purchased directly from coffee producers and farms from around the world. These relationships and Novo's commitment to quality ensures consistency and the subtle finetuning of bean flavor and espresso-machine performance. The company's Roastery on Larimer Street in RiNo is open to the public and hosts a number of coffee-making classes (brewing, milk steaming, seed-to-cup) and tours behind the scenes. They've aggregated a community of like-minded coffee enthusiasts, and they are enthusiastic proselytizers of coffee culture. Go to one of their regular, Friday-night tastings of different coffee styles, mixing up beans, roast levels, and brewing. Their cold brew is exceptional.

The Novo coffee shop location at Glenarm Place, off the Sixth Street Mall and across from the ornate, "Zig Zag Art Deco" Paramount Theater, is spacious and modern with high ceilings. All concrete and steel with sharp lines and bright colors, it has the vibe of a hipster art gallery. The most thoughtful touch is a metal foot rail along the bar for hooking your boot – and they serve only coffee. The main wall by the bar is a glassed garage door that opens wide on nice days. There are also four big tables of fenced-off outdoor seating, plus two more Novo locations in Highlands and Gilpin.

Address 1600 Glenarm Place, Denver, CO 80202, +1 (303) 295-7678, www.novocoffee.com/locations/glenarm | Getting there Bus 0, 6, 8, 19, 48 to 15th & Welton Streets | Hours Mon – Fri 6:30am – 5pm, Sat & Sun 7am – 4pm | Tip Whittier Café serves only African espresso and is known for its Ethiopian coffee ceremonies, held every Sunday at 2pm. Try the imported African beers and wines too (1710 E 25th Avenue, www.whittiercafe.com).

74 Omni Ballroom

If you can move, you can dance

Don't let the industrial zoning fool you. From the outside, this dance studio has all the charm of a repurposed warehouse… because that's what it is. That means there are hectares of hardwood floor space to shake your booty here. Match this ideal venue with a crew of dedicated, patient, and talented dance instructors, and you'll quickly gain new skills and confidence.

There are classes in every dance style you can think of, from Latin and swing to ballroom and country. Are you more drawn to the Lindy Hop? Check. Or is rumba your thing? Got that, too. There is real soul to this place. Joy abounds.

Dancing can also be very intimidating. It's vulnerable to let go and be moved by music, even more so with a partner. Many of us have performance anxiety from awkward childhood memories in stuffy gymnasiums. And this dance studio seems custom built to ease those traumas. Besides group or individual classes, you can also attend "social dancing" events that gently cater to getting everyone on the dancefloor, partnered or not.

The offerings also include fitness classes, plus private events, kids classes, and special performances. And in the spirit of "boldly going where everyone has gone before," adaptive classes for people with mobility restrictions are offered, too. Perhaps the sweetest class here is for couples about to get married. Omni Ballroom offers Wedding Preparation classes to help lovers about to stand before their community get comfortable with their first dance.

A smaller yet kindred spirit, the Mercury Café (2199 California Street) was first founded in 1975 and also caters to people with two left feet. Though not a dedicated dance studio, the Mercury Café offers dance classes in various styles. After evening classes, a DJ or a live band typically plays, and you're encouraged to show off your new moves. Thankfully, there's a full bar and food available.

Address 3800 S Jason Street, Englewood, CO 80110, +1 (720) 325-6305, www.omniballroom.org | Getting there Bus 51 to S Kalamath Street & W Lehigh Avenue | Hours See website for class schedule | Tip The Denver Turnverein was started by German immigrants in 1865 to "promote social well-being," including dance (1570 Clarkson Street, www.denverturnverein.com).

75_ Our Lady of Mount Carmel

The spiritual heart of Denver's Little Italy

Our Lady of Mount Carmel Catholic Church was constructed in the late 19th century basically because Denver's Irish Catholics and Italian Catholics hated each other. The Italians wanted their own church, where they could worship in peace, and raised the funds to make it happen. Instrumental in this effort was Rev. Father Felix Mariano Lepore, the church's founding priest. His first labor, a modest wood structure, burned down, so the community regrouped and constructed a proper church of brick and stucco. But in a plot sequence straight out of *The Sopranos*, Lepore was shot near the altar in 1903 when a debt dispute turned violent. Lepore allegedly owed the wrong people money and was killed by a hired gun sent to Denver by creditors in New York.

Our Lady of Mount Carmel's Romanesque revival-style building has since been placed on the National Register of Historic Places. The dual-tower edifice and silent, incense-bathed interior are much the same over a century on, but the surrounding neighborhood of Highland is a shell of its former self. Once known as Little Italy, this area in the hills northwest of downtown Denver was settled after the spring flood of 1864 that wiped out much of Denver, including "The Bottoms" along the South Platte River. The once-substantial Italian population here has since been assimilated.

People say that an entire generation of Italian immigrants here never learned to drive, because all they needed was right in this neighborhood – schools, shops, businesses, parks, and, at the heart of it all, Mount Carmel Church. Named after a sacred mountain in Israel, the church honors the mendicant Carmelite Order. Like any church, Mount Carmel has regular services and does charitable community outreach. But most importantly, the church hosts an annual bocce tournament, a good reason to consider converting to Catholicism.

Address 3549 Navajo Street, Denver, CO 80211, +1 (303) 455-0447,
www.ourladymountcarmel.com | Getting there Bus 19, 52 to Navajo Street &
W 35th Avenue | Hours See website for mass schedule | Tip Gaetano's Italian restaurant
was once a front for the mafioso Fat Paulie. People allegedly lost fingers in the basement.
The FBI bugged the place to root out gambling and loansharking (3760 Tejon Street,
www.gaetanositalian.com).

76__Patterson Inn

The city's most-haunted hotel

Built in 1891, the Croke-Patterson-Campbell Mansion is the site of several failed exorcisms, terrifying generations of priests along the way. Drawers open and close. There's a ghost of a past resident who committed suicide in the building. People reportedly hear phantom voices, self-typing typewriters, and crying babies in the basement. Jack Osborn even filmed an episode of *Portals to Hell* here (season 2, episode 7), declaring it legit haunted. Today, the building operates as a nine-room boutique hotel called the Patterson Inn, and spectrally sensitive travelers can book a room to experience communications from the supernatural. Or perhaps not.

The mansion's most famous resident was Thomas Macdonald Patterson, a US senator and congressman from Colorado. He cast an instrumental Electoral College vote in the Compromise of 1877, the contested election of President Rutherford B. Hayes, which effectively ended Reconstruction and ushered in the Jim Crow Era. Southern Democrats agreed to accept the Republican President if the Union pulled the last Union troops from the South, allowing self-governance again post-Civil War. Patterson went on to own the *Rocky Mountain News* and died in the building. Decades later, resident sisters regularly spotted his specter.

Built in the châteauesque architecture style, this hulking, sandstone building is perched on a rise above street level, which gives it a looming, castle-like presence. Weathered copper tops the roof's black-shingled spires, and magnificent rose bushes frame the imposing front stairs. The building has served as an orchestra school, radio station, private apartments, and offices over the years and earned National Register of Historic Places designation in 1973. It was also abandoned for long stretches before finally being renovated into a hotel in 2012. Now the ghosts aren't so lonely anymore.

Address 420 E 11th Avenue, Denver, CO 80203, +1 (303) 955-5142, www.pattersoninn.com, scott@pattersoninn.com | Getting there Bus 10 to 12th Avenue & Pennsylvania Street | Hours Open lobby hours | Tip The Stanley Hotel attracts its share of ghost hunters. Horror author Stephen King set his novel *The Shining* in an eerily familiar mountain hotel after a visit here (333 Wonderview Avenue, Estes Park, www.stanleyhotel.com).

77__Peak Thrift

Turning used clothes into social services for youth

Urban Peak provides supportive services to youths aged 15–24 who are experiencing homelessness. It's an absolutely vital resource for young people on Denver's streets, where they are vulnerable to human trafficking, violence, and drug abuse. You can support the important work of this stellar organization by shopping at Peak Thrift.

The thrift store is like any other that's supplied by a privileged community (i.e. they sell great stuff), except that it exclusively employs youth who have experienced homelessness or are at risk of homelessness. It's one of many programs at Urban Peak designed to provide "youth associates" with work experience and a safe place to forge healthy relationships. The store also provides these young people with shopping vouchers to help them purchase clothing and home essentials, as they secure housing, education, and other employment. All remaining profits get funneled back into Urban Peak's programs, which include an overnight youth shelter, street outreach, a day-time drop-in center, education and employment services, and housing.

Clothes shopping comes naturally to most people, and this place has a wide selection at low prices. Peak Thrift also accepts donations, of course, so head here with your surplus clothes and household items – even camping and outdoor equipment. The store's youth associates run an efficient, tight ship, and the more experienced employees teach the newcomers self-sufficiency in a supportive environment.

Peak Thrift is an exceptional learning tool that helps heal the trauma associated with homelessness and its causes, by empowering youth. Trauma impacts every area of human functioning, and the trauma-informed care provided by staff recognizes and acknowledges this. By simply shopping here, you can make lasting, positive impacts on multiple levels for the approximately 2,000 youth Urban Peak serves annually.

Address 4890 Pecos Street, Denver, CO 80221, +1 (303) 974-2929, www.peakthrift.org, info@peakthrift.org | **Getting there** Bus 19 to Pecos Street & W 50th Avenue | **Hours** Sat & Sun 10am–2pm | **Tip** False Ego is Black-owned clothing store that sells hip, edgy streetwear. All production impacts are offset by planting trees in Tanzania, garment recycling, and sourcing sustainable fabrics (2650 Walnut Street, www.falseego.eco).

78 Plains Conservation Center

Grasslands in their natural state

The wind and solitude of the Plains Conservation Center remind of *My Antonia* by Willa Cather. The vast grasslands east of Denver are in the rain shadow of the Rockies, and it's easy to feel like a forlorn Nebraska homesteader when you scan the horizon. North America's east-moving storms dump moisture over the high mountains and are wrung out before hitting the Great Plains. But this sea of grass evolved in concert with grazing buffalo and has its own quiet rhythms. The periodic trampling by millions of buffalo aerated the soil and caused grasses to regenerate. Today, irrigation ditches diverting mountain runoff serve that purpose for agriculture. The High Line Canal was integral to Denver's early viability.

The Center is staffed by a biologist, who gamely traffics student groups and visitors. The building's open room of displays does fair justice to the Native American tribes that thrived here for millennia before European colonization. There are maps, tools, and informative displays that put local tribes into context. The Front Range was primarily the home of the Ute and Arapaho, who hunted buffalo on foot before horses were introduced to the continent in the 1500s. The truism that tribes used every part of the buffalo – from hides to bone to sinew – is underscored by the inflated bison bladder on display used as a water jug. There's a curved-blade mezzaluna food chopper made of steel, a major improvement over stone tools for butchering.

There's a maze of hiking trails across the 1,100-acre site, and the Center has purchased close to 9,000 acres in the state for conservation. Bring binoculars to grasp fully the scope of this place. It's also fun to spy the fighter jets circling overhead on their way to and from Buckley Airforce Base a short mile or two north. The Center also has a collection for historic farm equipment and four Cheyenne-style teepees.

Address 21901 E Hampden Avenue, Aurora, CO 80013, +1 (303) 693-3621, www.plainsconservationcenter.org | Getting there Bus 133 to S Ceylon Street & Hampden Avenue | Hours Mon–Fri 8am–4pm, Sat 9am–5pm | Tip Just four miles southeast, the Arapahoe County Fairgrounds and Park is a massive complex for showcasing rural Colorado. It neighbors a horse racing track and Aurora Reservoir (25690 East Quincy Avenue, Aurora, www.arapahoecountyeventcenter.com).

79_Podium Karting
Go in circles with maximum efficiency

This isn't the Indianapolis 500, but you can pretend it is. Racing cars on closed tracks is reserved for the wealthy few, and karting is a welcome equalizer. The over-powered lawnmowers at Podium Karting & Events hug corners like they're on rails and rent for reasonable prices. The quarter-mile indoor track is miniature, but the speeds feel greater than they are, your butt mere centimeters off the ground when racing. The professional race cars in the soaring, glass atrium entry are nice nods to the fine engineering that underpins the sport.

The karts top out at 45 miles per hour, but average lap speeds don't exceed much above 30 miles per hour. As you zip through the 12 turns, chicanes, and switchbacks, improving performance quickly becomes addictive. The fear of crashing into the plastic safety barriers can be limiting at first, but your confidence builds quickly. After a few laps, ripping through the course becomes soothingly familiar. Increased efficiency is palpable in the din of screaming motors. Squeezing tiny degrees of speed becomes a compulsion. The trick is maintaining consistent speed. Drastic deceleration, skidding, or heaven forbid, spinning out, reduces overall efficiency.

Races last approximately 10 minutes, good for seven or eight laps. Helmeted participants complete a minimum of two races and adhere to a set of colored flags that race marshals wave to communicate when drivers need to slow down, move over, or stop. Each kart is fitted with a chip, and lap times are meticulously recorded. Comparing your time to other racers is part of the fun. Up to 10 drivers are allowed on-track per race, so unless you've rented out the facility, you'll be going against other parties. A former car dealership, the building is a cement monstrosity, with generous space for large groups. There's even a bar and axe-throwing for entertainment.

Address 7300 Broadway, Denver, CO 80221, +1 (720) 282-5000, www.podiumkarting.com | Getting there Bus 8 to Broadway & Bronco Road | Hours Mon–Thu noon–9pm, Fri noon–11pm, Sat 9am–11pm, Sun 9am–7pm | Tip High Plains Raceway is an amateur racetrack where car and motorcycle owners can test their skills in "open" track sessions. A dizzying selection of race classes compete here too (93301 E Highway 36, Deer Trail, www.highplainsraceway.com).

80 __ Riverside Cemetery
Dead men do tell tales

Founded in 1876, Riverside is Denver's oldest cemetery still in operation. There were nondescript "boot hills" prior, with pitiful grave markers for the anonymous, but the local elite wanted to be remembered with proper headstones. The notable dead here include early pioneers and civic luminaries, and because the West has always attracted immigrants, many graves here mark foreign-born Denverites. Chin Lin Sou (1837–1894) was a Chinese community leader who founded six companies. Park Hee Byung (1871–1907) was a Korean-born political organizer.

One of the more heartbreaking graves is that of Silas Soule (1839–1865). You may see flowers and mementos on the resting place for this principled hero in section 27 among Colorado's Civil War dead. Soule was an abolitionist and a "conductor" for the Underground Railroad in Kansas, helping people escaping enslavement to travel between safehouses to freedom. His political advocacy and prison breaks put his life in danger, so he moved to Colorado where he joined the Colorado First Regiment and helped repel a Confederate invasion at the Battle of Glorieta Pass (1862). Soule was promoted to Captain in the Colorado Cavalry for his cool under fire. He went on to become police marshal of Denver.

Soule tried to avert the Sand Creek Massacre in 1864, lobbying against the military expedition from Denver and ordering his troops not to fire on the peaceful encampment of Cheyenne and Arapaho. But John Chivington, the leader of this unprovoked attack (derisively known as the "Butcher of Sand Creek" until his death), was enraged by Soule's insubordination. Two gunmen tricked Soule into a Denver alley one year later and gunned him down. He was just 26 years old and had been walking home with his wife, whom he'd married three weeks earlier. Chivington was suspected to have ordered the assassination, but nothing was ever proved.

FATHER

陸 永 元

LOOK WING YUEN
1845 — 1908

Address 5201 Brighton Boulevard, Denver, CO 80216, www.friendsofriversidecemetery.org | Getting there Bus 48 to 48th Avenue & York Street; RTD Rail to Brighton National Western Center Station (N Line) | Hours Daily 9am–5pm | Tip A plaque in Skyline Park marks the spot where Silas Soule was killed. It's a hard reminder of his heroic stand for justice and the ignorance that underpins hate (15th Street & Arapahoe Avenue).

81 Rockmount Ranch Wear
Birthplace of Western-style clothing

Most people don't realize that Western clothing was, in fact, invented by a single man from Denver. Jack Weil designed the Western shirt in the 1940s by pulling from cowboy culture. The button snaps, shoulder yokes, and stiff collar are for ranch work. The heavier material and extra reinforcements made the shirts tougher, and the snaps were safer, as buttons can catch on ropes or saddle leather. The design caught on and has since proliferated across the world.

Affectionately called Papa Jack, Weil started Rockmount Ranch Wear in 1946 and built his business on the back of his shirts, as it were. He worked daily until passing at 107 years old, and his family runs the business to this day. It's fitting that Rockmount Ranch Wear is housed in a 100-year-old brick building in the heart of LoDo because Western clothing has become a form of living history. Wazee Street is as durable and authentically Western as the cowboy.

"The West is not a place," Weil was fond of saying. "It's a state of mind." His shirts are distinctive, living artifacts of Americana. Actors and musicians have long taken to wearing Rockmount designs in a grab for this authenticity. The Rockmount website has an entire page devoted to celebrities wearing the brand, everyone from Elvis Presley and Macklemore to Jack Black and Salvador Dali. A Rockmount shirt can even be found on display at the Smithsonian.

Don a brimmed hat, heeled leather boots, jeans with a proper belt buckle, and a snap shirt, and any man, woman, or child can feel a pride that's distinctly American (mustache optional). You instantly assume the tough, no-nonsense persona of the cowboy, whether you run cattle or not. Papa Jack is as responsible as anyone for perpetuating this mystique. Stetson hats or Tony Lama boots may have more brand recognition, but Rockmount is absolutely foundational to the cachet of the American West.

Address 1626 Wazee Street, Denver, CO 80202, +1 (800) 776-2566, www.rockmount.com | **Getting there** Bus Mall Ride to 16th Street Mall & Wazee Street | **Hours** Mon–Fri 8am–5pm, Sat 10am–6pm, Sun 11am–4pm | **Tip** Want a cowboy hat that will last a lifetime? Coleen Orr at Cowboy Up Hatters uses traditional techniques to shape the most authentic, durable hats in North Denver (by appointment only, www.cowboyuphatters.com).

82 Rocky Mountain Arsenal
War then peace in the grasslands

A former chemical weapons manufacturing facility, Rocky Mountain Arsenal National Wildlife Refuge is a sterling example of environmental remediation done right. For 50 years (1942–1992) US Army personnel worked here to cook up increasingly horrific ways to kill people. A deadly suite of war chemicals was perfected here: sarin, mustard gas, napalm, white phosphorus, chlorine gas, and lewisite. Yet, incredibly, this 16,000-acre refuge is essentially wildland today.

Most of the buildings have been removed, the soil remediated, and native plants nurtured. The federal government, US military, the State of Colorado, and the petrochemical industry collaborated to pay for the cleanup, although a 12,000-foot "deep injection well" (sealed off since the 1960s) still contains a poisonous witch's brew.

Just eight miles from downtown, this refuge is a lovely parkland today. More than 330 species of animals roam about here, including bison, raptors, black-footed ferrets, coyotes, deer, and white pelicans. It's a strange juxtaposition to enjoy the peace and wildlife, knowing that chemicals now banned by international treaties were produced here. These chemicals killed many thousands of troops and civilians in America's wars (explicit and clandestine) to combat the spread of communism in Southeast Asia and beyond. This facility was also used to house German World War II prisoners of war.

Denver's strategic location in the geographic middle of the US made this location virtually impossible to attack. The defensibility of this locked remoteness is why the North American Air Defense Command (NORAD) is buried deep in mountains west of Colorado Springs. That's where fingers hover over The Button, threatening and therefore keeping us from nuclear annihilation, or so the logic goes. NORAD also tracks the annual flight of Santa Claus on Christmas Eve, an odd, enduring American tradition.

Address 6550 Gateway Road, Commerce City, CO 80022, +1 (303) 289-0930, www.fws.gov/refuge/rocky-mountain-arsenal | **Getting there** Bus 65 to Central Park Boulevard & 54th Avenue | **Hours** Daily dawn–dusk, Visitor Center Wed–Sun 9am–4pm | **Tip** Rocky Flats National Wildlife Refuge is another former Superfund-site-turned-refuge. This former nuclear weapons production facility paid massive fines for illegal pollution and faced class-action suits for allegedly causing cancer to employees (10801 Highway 93, Golden, www.fws.gov/refuge/Rocky_Flats).

83 Ruby Hill

World-class bike park

Ruby Hill in south Denver was once used by Native Americans as a lookout for hunting buffalo. It's easy to see why – the 360-degree views from this spot reach from Pikes Peak to Longs Peak, from the jagged Boulder Flatirons and Continental Divide to the hazy plains and downtown skyline. Come winter, this spot is also Denver's best sledding hill. Kids in ski pants and warm boots swarm here on snow days, saucers in tow. In the summer, the community garden (managed in collaboration with D.U.G. Denver Urban Gardens) overflows with color and abundant produce.

Gold-fevered miners in the mid-1800s discovered what they thought were rubies on this rise above the South Platte River. Even though the red-hued gems turned out to be common garnets, the name Ruby Hill stuck. The land that's now the Ruby Hill Park was a landfill until 1968, when the city thought better and bought it, transforming the hilltop of rubbish into the grand green space it is today.

2016 was a big year for the park, when construction began for the Levitt Pavilion and the imaginative Ruby Hill Mountain Bike Park. Levitt Pavilion presents more than 50 free concerts and events annually. Bring your lawn chairs and blankets – no seating here, just sloping lawn.

Up the hill in a dedicated area, the Ruby Hill Mountain Bike Park, also free, challenges riders of all levels to experience gravity in surprising new ways. The smooth and undulating pump tracks allow riders to use their momentum and body movement to roll through the course without pedaling. The skills course includes rock causeways, ladder bridges, and banked turns for more technical riding, and the dirt jumps have helpful transitions for practicing big air. The slopestyle course is a crowning achievement. The series of fabricated ramps and wall rides, berms, rollers, and tabletop jumps are outrageously fun and only semi-dangerous.

Address 1200 W Florida Avenue, Denver, CO 80223, www.rubyhilldenver.com | Getting there Bus 21 to W Evans Avenue & S Lipan Street | Hours Daily dawn–dusk | Tip Valmont Bike Park is another marvel of sculptural engineering. The trails and various courses, jumps, and pump tracks are designed to hurl you forward across 42 acres (3160 Airport Road, Boulder, www.bouldercolorado.gov/locations/valmont-bike-park).

84 Rupp's Drums
The beat goes strong

Devotion to a single instrument can be a spiritual experience. Drums are already hypnotic by nature, and no matter how fluent your expression becomes, the layers of potential rhythm and time signatures are fractal. Practicing drums is a form of surrender to this mathematical infinity – play the drums, and the drums play you. Rupp's Drums has been helping professional and amateur drummers explore these riddles and rhythms for 36 years.

Bob Rupp started the business from his living room before expanding into the current location, a cozy, former single-family home. He was always adamant about collaborating with professional drummers to offer clinics, which stoked excitement with his client base. For instance, he somehow roped in the infamously cantankerous Ginger Baker (Cream) for a workshop. Touring musicians stop by all the time to resupply because this is only one of five remaining dedicated drum stores in the nation. The store's wall of fame is crammed with signed pictures of professional drummers, like jazz-fusion virtuoso Dennis Chambers (Santana, Parliament/Funkadelic), Ryan Brown (Dweezil Zappa), and Todd Sucherman (Styx).

The store's current ownership is adamant that all employees must be gigging drummers. The staff's collective experience spans many, many decades and pleasantly informs your shopping for new and used hand drums, acoustic drums, ritual drums, and electronic drums, plus parts, repairs, and rentals. The Upbeat Drum School uses two lesson rooms at the back of the building, and there's a padded, cordoned-off demo room for wailing away on drums before purchase.

It's strangely satisfying to examine a $10,000 drum kit or a wall of drumsticks, but the room of cymbals is otherworldly. Soft red lighting suffuses the small space, reflecting off racks and racks of cymbals. The golden discs levitate from floor to ceiling like alien plants, belying the tones and crashes they can produce.

Address 2045 S Holly Street, Denver, CO 80222, +1 (303) 756-5777, www.ruppsdrums.com, rupp@ruppsdrums.com | **Getting there** Bus 21 to Evans Avenue & S Holly Street | **Hours** Tue–Fri 10am–6pm, Sat 11am–5pm, Sun noon–4pm | **Tip** Guitar geeks worship at Flipside Music. The variety of new and used guitars, amplifiers, and effects equipment is archival (1673 S Acoma Street, www.flipside-music.com).

85 — Sacred Thistle

Meditative artistry as home decor

Is your collection of "house blessings" as complete as it could be? Sidney and Cornelia Peterson, the mother-daughter duo that runs this shop, both went to art school, and it shows. Step into their thoughtfully curated space, and the *objets d'art*, flowers, ceramics, perfume, and more create a centered, balanced feeling. And also lust. Hold on to your wallet – leaving here without purchasing more than you intended is basically impossible. If the jewelry and totes don't get you, the beeswax candles and wooden serving utensils will.

The Peterson's space has the quiet feel of an art gallery, as the store's displays take on an almost sculptural aspect in aggregate. The collections inhabit the 100-year-old brick building like they were purpose-made to offset each other's textures. Take your time to wander the creaky wood floors and ogle the glass case of seashells, or caress the colorful wall of impossibly soft Pendleton blankets. Dab yourself with luxurious skin care, or inhale the spicy aromas of incense. The display of art books showcases remarkable tomes that will become family heirlooms.

The cut flower arrangements are tableaux of strange shapes and colors. You can purchase roses by the dozen, but Sacred Thistle is where to go if the Japanese art of *ikebana* is your thing. There's a small forest of tall cacti and euphorbia by the sunny front windows. The spineless "chocolate drop" Euphorbia Candelabra for $1,025 is taller than a man. Native to Rhodesia, these grow impossibly slowly, and large specimens are rare. Its star-shaped spines and a bluish green hue are otherworldly.

Walk outside and around the corner to see the proudly purple, building-wide mural by AJ Davis. The kaleidoscopic shapes and animals gleefully liven up the typically drab, urban parking lot. And across the street a colossal steel cow and her calf tower above the walkway to the Denver Museum of Modern Art.

Address 1110 Acoma Street, Denver, CO 80210, +1 (720) 598-6957, www.sacredthistle.com | Getting there Bus 52 to Bannock Street & W 11th Avenue | Hours Mon–Sat 11am–6pm, Sun noon–5pm | Tip Sam McNeil at Superior Iron Works Plus will make you a bouquet of flowers from steel. The man is a genius at recycling discarded metal into art (2630 Arapahoe Street, www.siwplus.com).

86 __ Sakura Square
Colorado's Japanese American heritage

Just two months after the attack on Pearl Harbor in 1941, President Franklin Delano Roosevelt signed the infamous Executive Order 9066. This relegated approximately 112,000 people of Japanese ancestry, 70,000 of whom were American citizens, to prison camps across the West. One such camp was in southeastern Colorado. The Granada War Relocation Center housed more than 7,000 men, women, and children, mostly citizens. Incredibly, more than 400 Japanese-American men from the camp later volunteered for the US military to fight the Japanese, Germans, and Italians in World War II.

Many from the camp relocated to Denver after the war and formed organizations like the Tri-State/Denver Buddhist Temple around the corner from Sakura Square, a roughly one square-block of downtown Denver dedicated to celebrating and preserving Colorado's Japanese-American heritage, culture, and community. The statues and meditative garden on the southwest corner memorialize the shameful imprisonment resulting from Executive Order 9066 – and the heroes who fought against dehumanizing others, including Colorado's Governor at the time, Ralph L. Carr.

On the east side of the block, Pacific Mercantile Company (www.pacificeastwest.com) sells an impressive array of Japanese products, ingredients, and authentic cookware. If you've ever wanted to make your own sushi or ramen, this is your one-stop shop. In classic Japanese style, the employees are extremely helpful and open to guiding you through the aisles to help translate. It's a disorienting yet lovely experience to be completely surrounded by indecipherable Japanese and Asian characters.

Also on that block, make a point of finding the immense iron bell outside the Buddhist Temple. It has its own pagoda-like pavilion and a suspended log for striking. The bell is struck at ceremonial times, and the deep resonance penetrates your body.

Address 1255 19th Street, Denver, CO 80202, +1 (303) 295-0305, www.sakurasquare.com |
Getting there Bus 38, 52 to Larimer & 19th Streets | Hours Unrestricted | Tip Pacific
Ocean Marketplace is a powerhouse of Asian cuisine. The selection of produce and seafood
is exotic and impressive (2200 W Alameda Avenue, www.pacificoceanmarket.com).

87 __ Samana Float Center
Alter your state

Floating in an isolation tank can be compared to lying supine on a soft bed, soaking wet in total darkness. The shallow water in each tank is impossibly dense, thanks to 1,100 pounds of dissolved magnesium sulfate (Epsom salts), creating a firm, liquid cushion. Floating is effortless and requires zero input from the floater. Just insert the wax earplugs and let yourself go.

At the Samana Float Center, the familiar spa formula of low lighting, soothing scents, and quiet music instantly puts you at ease. This is important, because the 90-minute isolation tank experience can make you feel slightly vulnerable. It requires trust to relax so completely, and the professional, intuitive staff here understands. They usher floaters through the experience like respectful monks.

The isolation pods, or "cabins," seem borrowed from a science fiction plot, designed for years-long travel through deep space. Also known as float tanks, float pods, or floatation tanks, isolation tanks were developed in 1954 by neuropsychiatrist John C. Lilly and gained some popularity through the 1970s before being dismissed as an oddity (no thanks to the 1980 movie, *Altered States*). But isolation tanks are much more than glorified hot tubs, and their resurgent credibility can be attributed to high-tech filtration and thorough hygienic practices – and because people love the experience.

The purported mental, physical, and creative benefits of 90-minute submersion in isolation tanks can seem hyperbolic, but there's no denying the strange and profoundly relaxing experience of floating on a cloud. It's like experiencing your mother's womb before you emerged. With nothing to process, the mind is released to feel itself, and the sensory deprivation somehow *heightens* the senses in their absence. Research has confirmed that the experience can help mitigate anxiety disorders and soothe muscle soreness.

Address 1307 26th Street, Denver, CO 80205, +1 (720) 573-8744, www.samanafloat.com, info@samanafloat.com | Getting there Bus 44 to Larimer & 26th Streets | Hours Daily 8am–9pm | Tip Havana Health Sauna is a traditional Korean spa with an amethyst and rose quartz meditation room for healing your soul (2020 S Havana Street, www.havanahealthsauna.com).

88__ Sarkisian's
The cave of wonders

The brothers who run Sarkisian's Rugs & Fine Art are fifth-generation rug merchants. Their great grandfather started the business in 1891, a claim very few Denver businesses can legitimately make. From museum quality to curious novelties, the exotic treasures at Sarkisian are densely packed and somewhat overwhelming. It's hard to know where to look, because every piece is arresting. The original Sarkisian was a rug merchant in Armenia, who sent his kids to America to escape genocide by the Turks. His grandson, H. Medill Sarkisian, was so enamored by his family's legacy that he earned a degree in Asian studies from University of Colorado and advanced degrees from Harvard and Colorado College. This Sarkisian spoke seven languages fluently and was an internationally recognized expert in Chinese and Persian weaving. He traveled the globe annually to source the finest rugs for display in Denver.

Piled deep and high, precious Asian artifacts have been cycling through this building since the 1940s. H. Medill Sarkisian's wife grew weary of her husband's collecting and compelled him to bring his treasures here or get a new wife. And so the business grew from selling just rugs to include fine art. Navigating the warren of rooms is akin to an archeological expedition.

You can find everything from brass surveying transits to Indonesian shadow puppets made from water buffalo hide. There's fine china, tapestries, statuary, swords, Japanese samurai armor, geodes, and much more. Look for an original gibbet. This human-shaped, iron body cage from 7th century England was used to encase unfortunate souls, who were then eviscerated and left to die – slowly. One man's object d'art is another man's medieval torture device.

The Denver Art Museum has an invaluable Sarkisian-donated Tang Dynasty (7th–10th century) ceramic ox-drawn cart on permanent display.

Address 693 E Speer Boulevard, Denver, CO 80203, +1 (303) 733-2623, www.sarkisian.com, info@sarkisian.com | Getting there Bus 3L, 83D, 83L to Speer Boulevard & Washington Street | Hours Tue–Sat 10am–5pm | Tip Lake Steam Baths offers traditional Russian and Turkish baths – sauna, steam room, salt scrubs – with dedicated days for men and women (3540 W Colfax Avenue, www.lakesteam.com).

89 Shambhala Center

Stronghold of Tibetan Buddhism

This large, stately stone building across from the rollicking Boulder Theater and just off the Pearl Street walking mall is home to the Shambala Center. Founded by the late Tibetan Lama Chögyam Trungpa Rinpoche in 1974, this organization pioneered the teaching of secular Buddhism in the West. His vision was to manifest the mythical, utopian Kingdom of Shambhala in real life. Though controversial for his teaching methods, Chögyam Trungpa Rinpoche hosted the 14th Dalai Lama on his visit to Boulder in 1981.

Today the Center offers in-person and online classes, including dharma talks, meditations, and recovery support, and support for marginalized groups. It's the spiritual anchor for many Buddhists along the Front Range. Walk-ins are welcome.

When Chögyam Trungpa Rinpoche first came to the United States in 1970, he met a willing public. Young Americans had been primed by the sexual, political, and cultural revolutions of the 1960s and were open to new ideas. Chögyam Trungpa Rinpoche was a respected monk and scholar in Tibet before escaping his homeland in 1959, when the Chinese invaded and destroyed his monastery. His teacher had prophesied that his star disciple would bring Buddhist teachings to the West, so the young monk fled, spending a year in hiding and several months crossing the Himalayas to reach India.

Chögyam Trungpa Rinpoche gave up monastic vows to become a lay teacher and was known for drinking alcohol, smoking cigarettes, and his sexual proclivities. But he had a knack for presenting esoteric religious philosophy and practices and was widely respected. Chögyam Trungpa Rinpoche founded more than 100 meditation centers around the world, including the 600-acre Shambhala Meditation Center in Red Feather Lakes, Colorado. He also founded the parent organization that started Boulder's Naropa University, the first Buddhist-accredited university in the US.

Address 1345 Spruce Street, Boulder, CO 80302, +1 (303) 444-0190,
www.boulder.shambhala.org | Getting there Bus FF1 to Downtown Boulder Station |
Hours Mon–Fri 1–6pm | Tip Celestial Seasonings was founded in 1969. This global
juggernaut of teas and herbal infusions offers tours of its state-of-the-art facility
(4600 Sleepytime Drive, Boulder, www.celestialseasonings.com).

90__The Sink

Confusing drunk college students for sport

Founded in 1876 before Colorado was even a state, the University of Colorado Boulder, or just "CU," is the flagship of the public University of Colorado system. The Buffs and student culture have long dominated life in Boulder and helped shape the restaurant and bar scene, especially on The Hill, the collection of businesses on 13th Street next to the university. The most iconic bar/restaurant on the Hill, The Sink has operated here under various names since 1923. It's home to a fantastic selection of burgers and whimsical items, like Ugly Crust pizzas. (The P.O.T.U.S. is named after President Obama, who dined here in 2012, and built his own with pepperoni, sausage, green peppers, olives, and mozzarella.)

The famously low ceilings and exposed, head-smashing pipes have caused a lot of headaches. But that didn't stop celebrity chefs Guy Fieri and Anthony Bourdain from stopping by to record episodes for their television shows. Over time, a crew of "Beatnik artists" painted the interior in weird murals, and today every square inch of wall space is covered in graffiti. Look for the image of Robert Redford, who attended CU for a year in 1955 to play baseball, working at The Sink as a janitor. The effect creates an off-balance optical illusion that makes navigating the cramped interior a bit challenging, especially after a few drinks.

Beware of the wall that's painted to look exactly like the entrance to the men's room. It's a time-honored tradition to sit near this faux doorway and watch tipsy freshmen mistake the mural for the actual men's room. It's common to see guys plow straight into the wall.

The menu is enormous and exhaustive, with everything from Buff wings and French onion soup to roasted butternut squash salad and grilled salmon sandwiches. But the burgers are over-the-top succulent. The Hangover Cure and the Bourbon Jalapeño burgers are presidential too.

Address 1165 13th Street, Boulder, CO 80302, +1 (303) 444-7465, www.thesink.com, contact@thesink.com | **Getting there** Bus 204, 225, 225D, 22ND to Broadway & University Avenue | **Hours** Daily 11am–10pm | **Tip** The Dark Horse is a dark warren of confusing corners and hallways, not to mention the bizarre collection of carts and wagons that hang from the ceiling. The sign on the men's room door points to the women's room and vice versa. Awkward encounters guaranteed (2922 Baseline Road, Boulder, www.darkhorsebar.com).

91 Ski Lift Designs
Repurposed lift chairs as furniture

Where there are skiers, there are old skis. Drive through any Colorado ski town, and you'll eventually see a fence made of skis. Indulge in some raucous après ski at a Colorado ski resort, and you'll come across the omnipresent shot ski – a ski with affixed shot glasses for simultaneous, group consumption. As such, stroll through Denver's neighborhoods, and you'll see chairs and benches made from repurposed ski lift chairs.

Ski Lift Designs is a custom furniture maker in Englewood that specializes in this particular subgenre of furnishings. They purchase old ski lift chairs and then sandblast, galvanize, and paint them. The resulting benches look great outdoors and can be hung from decks or metal frames to simulate the feeling of being whisked up a mountain. It's a snow-specific niche, but skiers pay handsomely for these works of usable art.

Stop by Ski Lift Designs to see the impressive collection of finished furniture and their cool workshop with pieces in progress. These chairs are not reproductions but pieces of ski history. There's a private pleasure knowing your furniture had a previous life hauling skiers and snowboarders to their happy place. The Riblet center-post chair swings are particularly chic.

Ski Lift Designs is just one of several area businesses (Breck Ironworks in Breckenridge, for instance) that specializes in this type of nostalgic fetishizing. People lust for talismans of snowbound life. Think: Adirondack chairs made from skis, benches made from snowboards, and swings made from old ski lift chairs. Everything is sourced from decommissioned ski lifts from resorts around North America. The Denver office of Facebook/Meta proudly displays a Ski Lift Designs ski-lift bench in the lobby, backed by a wall of snow-capped peaks and blue sky. It's a selfie magnet. Got a spare $35,000? The refurbished Mammoth Mountain gondola is for you.

Address 2936 S Zuni Street, Unit E, Englewood, CO 80110, +1 (720) 391-5510, www.skiliftdesigns.com, support@skiliftdesigns.com | Getting there Bus 35 to W Dartmouth Avenue & S Zuni Street | Hours Mon–Fri 9am–5pm | Tip Colorado Ski Furniture specializes in Adirondack chairs made from old skis. Select your own skis from their pile and have a custom chair built to your style (419 Manitou Avenue, Manitou Springs, www.coloradoskichairs.com).

92 Snöbahn

Ski indoors without flying to Dubai

Skiing and snowboarding are not the most intuitive sports. The act of strapping planks to your feet and hurling yourself down an avalanche-prone mountain goes against basic survival instincts. If not learned in childhood, these sports can take years to perfect, especially if practiced infrequently. Travel to the mountains is expensive and so is all the specialized equipment and clothing. Risk of injury is also well-documented. The words "spiral fracture" are painful even just in print.

The trick to mastering the pull of gravity on snow-covered mountains is edging, or pushing the metal edges of your skis or snowboard into the snow. The sensory feedback loop of slowing your descent with edging, then allowing yourself to slide, is difficult to feel without trial and error, i.e. falling. This is where Snöbahn comes in.

The genius employed here is not fake snow on an indoor mountain, á la Dubai, but rolling treadmills. Developed in the Netherlands, the Maxxtracks "ski-slope simulators" are essentially gigantic versions of the regular treadmills from your local gym. They are covered with a slippery white surface, and skiers and snowboarders face downhill, remaining in place as the slope slips by underfoot. You learn edging by playing with balance, leaning forward and side to side, and feeling the grip of your edges – all in comfortable temperatures and very safe conditions.

This facility takes it even further with an indoor ramp for practicing jumps into a foam pit and various trampolines and bungie setups for practicing aerials. Parents or partners can chill on couches and sip adult beverages or coffee, while their loved ones receive instruction. There's even an indoor area for learning to skateboard on ramps and half-pipes. Snöbahn also has a convenient rental program for on-snow equipment and monthly memberships. Their slogan, "Long runs, no lines," sums it up perfectly.

Address 6955 S York Street, Centennial, CO 80122, +1 (303) 872-8494, www.snobahn.com | Getting there Bus 24, 66 to S University Boulevard & Commons Avenue | Hours Mon–Fri 10am–9pm, Sat & Sun 8am–8pm | Tip The Denver Curling Center has a dedicated building (and full bar) devoted to the obscure sport of sliding smooth stones across polished ice (14100 W 7th Street, Golden, www.denvercurlingclub.com).

93__ The Source

Food-hall chic

This brick and timber building was originally the Colorado Iron Works plant, which bellowed steam and belched steel from the 1870s through the mid-1900s. Down I-25, Pueblo, Colorado, may have been known as Steel City for its massive production volumes, but Denver was an industrial hub from day one and remains so. There's something bizarrely charming (if smelly and environmentally damaging) about having an oil refinery at the north end of town in Commerce City.

Historically, the River North neighborhood had many bustling manufacturing warehouses, which have now become the building blocks and mural canvases for the area's funky revival. Colorado Iron Works mainly produced ore-milling equipment and shipped the machinery worldwide.

Dilapidated railroad tracks used for freight trains can still be found out the back door. The Source Market Hall has incorporated old pieces from the foundry's history into the building's modern redesign, most importantly retaining the cavernous space, vaulted ceiling, and skylights.

There's a total of 45,000 square feet of market hall space and about 25 vendors, including several restaurants, a butcher, a florist, and an old-school barbershop. The focus is definitely "artisan," but you can do weekly shopping here when your supermarket routine gets old. Reunion Bread Co., for example, is an authentically dedicated baker, creating the finest bread crust and pastries imaginable. The market hall's open layout promotes interaction, naturally fostering a community feeling.

In contrast to the market hall, the "design-forward" Source Hotel next door is pleasingly modern – all glass and cement. The view from the roof-top deck of Woods restaurant and beer garden is spectacular. The Continental Divide feels so close you can touch it.

Address 3330 Brighton Boulevard, Denver, CO 80216, +1 (720) 443-1135, www.thesourcehotel.com/markethall | Getting there Bus 48 to Brighton Boulevard & 33rd Street | Hours Fri & Sat 6–2am, Sun–Thu 6am–midnight | Tip Denver Central Market is around the corner and has a very similar feel to the Source. Smaller, this high-end food court has excellent and varied food vendors, couches for chilling, and a craft-cocktail bar (2669 Larimer Street, www.denvercentralmarket.com).

94 Southwest Gardens

A soothing oasis of desert plants

The first thing you notice as you walk in the door is the smell: musty and fragrant, a lot like stepping off a plane in the tropics. The air here is softer somehow, enveloping and welcoming. The next thing you notice is that customers and staff speak in mellow tones. Southwest Gardens inspires the kind of reverence associated with museums. It's subconscious, but you cannot wander among these sculptural desert plants without feeling a pull in your chest. It's an otherworldly experience to bathe yourself in the peaceful silence of rows and rows of baby plants in their myriad pastel hews.

The cultivation of rare and exotic cacti and succulents is half science, half art, and 100% experience. As the saying goes, "Good judgment comes from experience, and experience comes from bad judgment." Cary West had the intelligence and patience to learn slowly how to nurture plants (orchids were his first love) and was foolhardy enough to open Southwest Gardens in 1989. Denver-born and bred, West attended Denver's North High, where he discovered his affinity for plants by growing them for scientific experiments. He never knew anything different and hasn't looked back.

West started his own nursery because he couldn't find the unique plants he wanted. Today, his horticultural haven is well worn, and each staff member is more knowledgeable than the next. Look for the illustrated poster with a fun illustration of West himself. Of course, you can also choose from immense stacks of cool pottery for displaying your cacti and succulents and stock up on organic fertilizers, garden tools, and much more, including your typical annuals, perennials, herbs, houseplants, and vegetables. Or take all the time you'd like and meander about.

Out back, under drooping foliage, you'll find a set of rickety garden furniture for relaxing. This is also where the nursery's immense cat will find you for a snuggle.

Address 4114 N Harlan Street, Wheatridge, CO 80033, +1 (303) 423-5606, www.southwestgardensco.com | Getting there Bus 44, 51 to W 44th Avenue & Harlan Street | Hours Daily 9am – 4pm | Tip Also founded in the late 1980s, Old Santa Fe Pottery is *the* place in Denver for Mexican folk décor, delicious hot sauces, and funky outdoor sculptures (2485 S Santa Fe Drive, www.santafe-pottery.com).

95 _ *Spirit*
The majestic bronze of Red Rocks Amphitheater

Fifteen feet tall and weighing 1,500 pounds, *Spirit* is the bronze likeness of Colorado's dear John Denver by American sculptor Sue DiCicco. The 1970s folk singer, songwriter, environmental activist (né Henry John Deutschendorf in New Mexico) is immortalized with flowing hair, an eagle landing on his forearm, and a guitar slung over his shoulder. Located near the front gate of Red Rocks Amphitheater, *Spirit* marks the location of the Colorado Music Hall of Fame in the adobe Trading Post building. Denver played 17 shows here, and his anthem "Rocky Mountain High" is one of two official state songs. He and Red Rocks Amphitheater itself were the first inductees into the Colorado Music Hall of Fame in 2012.

Besides *Spirit*, the coolest exhibit in the Colorado Music Hall of Fame showcases the incredibly prolific recording studio Caribou Ranch. The historic photos capture the diverse legends who recorded smash hits at 8,500 feet near Nederland, Colorado – everyone from Michael Jackson and Elton John to Frank Zappa and Al Di Meola.

Just 10 miles west of downtown, the geological wonder of Red Rocks Amphitheater has a well-deserved reputation for superb acoustics and glorious sunsets. Hewed from the local sandstone in the late 1930s by the Civilian Conservation Corps (CCC) and the Works Progress Administration (WPA), this naturally formed amphitheater opened to the public in 1941. It has a legitimate claim to being the best outdoor concert venue in the United States.

The entire Red Rocks property is a park that encompasses 868 acres. A trail system winds through the 200-million-year-old rocks. The area's sandstone originally took shape as sand dunes on the shores of an inland sea and contains fossilized dinosaur tracks and brontosaurus bones. Red Rocks' eponymous stone slabs were pushed up to the strange angles seen today by the very formation of the Rocky Mountains.

Address 18300 W Alameda Parkway, Morrison, CO 80465, +1 (720) 865-2494, www.redrocksonline.com | Getting there By car, take I-70 to Exit 259 towards County Road 93 and follow the signs to Red Rocks Park | Hours Daily 9am–5pm, see website for concert times | Tip Bandimere Speedway hosts drag races on a quarter-mile track. The profusion of race-car classes have two things in common: speed and insanely loud engines. Bring ear plugs, or risk going deaf (3051 S Rooney Road, Morrison, www.bandimere.com).

96 _ Stanley Marketplace

Aviation history transformed

Stanley Marketplace is on the former grounds of Stapleton International Airport, Denver's original airport. In operation from 1929 – 1995, the airport's terminals and buildings have been removed or repurposed, but you can still see the distinctive air traffic control tower that remains standing.

A defining fixture of northwest Aurora, it's a cool retro accent to the neighboring condominium developments. (It's also worth noting that the former Denver mayor and namesake of Stapleton International Airport was an open member of the Ku Klux Klan. The area's revitalization is a very welcome update.) The Stanley Marketplace itself is housed in the former facilities of Stanley Aviation, an aerospace company best known for developing innovative ejection seats for the military's then-new supersonic jets.

The marketplace is a collection of about 50 businesses – everything from restaurants and a brewery to a cutlery store and a karate dojo. Kids will love the classes at Bounce Gymnastics too. The bright signage and general design of the Stanley Marketplace is loud and proud. Industrial and playful, the tables at Japanese restaurant Misaki perfectly capture the Art Deco aesthetic. They make use of old bicycles, a once-functional motorcycle, and a vintage Vespa scooter to support the tabletops. The fresh sushi isn't bad either.

The Hangar event space is a former operational airplane hangar that opens, via immense sliding doors, onto what was once a private runway where Stanley Aviation conducted flight testing. This cavernous room hosts all kinds of music performances and events, and an outdoor tented pavilion hosts summer concerts on the grass. An extensive network of trails and greenspaces wind through the surrounding neighborhoods, so wear your best walking shoes and bring your dog along. Big outdoor sculptures and lawns invite people to lounge about if that's what's called for on a sunny day.

Address 2501 Dallas Street, Aurora, CO 80010, +1 (720) 990-6743, www.stanleymarketplace.com | Getting there Bus 20, 105 to Mountainview Boulevard & Clinton Street | Hours Thu–Sat 7am–9pm, Sun–Wed 7am–10pm | Tip Rosetta Hall in Boulder is much smaller but has a similar feeling. The historic building, open floor plan, and multiple restaurants makes for a communal food court (1109 Walnut Street, Boulder, www.rosettahall.com).

97 _ Stranahan's Whiskey
May your snifter runneth over

George Stranahan was a physicist, rancher, founder of Flying Dog Brewery, and father of nine. When you're smart and heir to the Champion Spark Plug fortune, good things can happen. Stranahan teamed with his Woody Creek, Colorado, neighbor Jess Graber to create Stranahan's Whiskey in 2004, Denver's first commercial distillery since Prohibition. Their collaboration has spawned a Golden Age of spirits locally. The Block Distilling (2990 Larimer Street, Denver) and State 38 Distilling (400 Corporate Circle, Golden) come to mind, along with many more up and down the Front Range.

This is high-quality, middle-shelf whiskey, which is why it's found in nearly every bar and liquor store in the nation. It's made with just four ingredients: malted barley, yeast, water, and charred oak barrels. Like Colorado itself, Stranahan's Whiskey is somehow simple and natural. It's easy to snuggle with a snifter of this stuff.

Every whiskey the company produces is distilled, aged, and bottled at this Denver location, a former printing press and brewery. To start, 60,000 pounds of barley are delivered every week! Mostly Colorado-grown, the barley is toasted in batches at different temperatures and rates, then blended. This creates a final mixture of toasted barleys integral to the brand's distinct flavor profile. After fermenting, the spent barley is sold to cattle ranchers for feed by the truckload.

The shimmering copper stills are strange, bulbous works of art, with pipes emanating at every angle. Stranahan's Whiskey is distilled twice to achieve the perfect flavor, then blended with fresh spring water from nearby Eldorado Springs to achieve the desired proof.

Excellent tour guides explain the process from start to finish and demonstrate proper whiskey-tasting technique in multiple rounds. Ruminate over your newfound knowledge afterwards in the comfortable Lounge bar.

Address 200 S Kalamath Street, Denver, CO 80223, +1 (303) 296-7440, www.stranahans.com |
Getting there Bus 0 to S Broadway & W Alameda Avenue; RTD Rail to Alameda (E Line) |
Hours Fri–Sun noon–8pm, Mon & Thu 3–8pm | Tip Leopold Bros is an impressive
distillery that produces a slew of spirits, including exceptional whiskeys, and offers informative
tours (5285 Joliet Street, www.leopoldbros.com).

98__ Street Intervention
Graffiti as playful protest

Walk the streets of the RiNo Art District, and you'll come across the paintings and stencil work of Belgian artist Jaune (@jaune_art). Tiny characters can be seen "working" on whimsical projects along Brighton Avenue, showering under a drainpipe or climbing on bricks. This particular work depicts two workers tossing a grappling hook up to a faucet. The shadow cast by the line and hook form a pleasing *trompe-l'oeil.*

"I'm addressing the lower-income jobs that make society work," says Jaune, who chose Denver as one of only four cities in the US to display his characters. "We pass workers every day, but we don't really notice them."

The world-class mural art in this part of town has transformed the streets and alleys into permanent, open-air galleries that value the shared human experience. Reminiscent of San Francisco's revitalized South of Market (SoMa) neighborhood, the RiNo Art District encompasses parts of four historical North Denver neighborhoods: Globeville, Elyria-Swansea, Five Points, and Cole. The area is rapidly evolving from an industrial zone into a walking-friendly hub for breweries, restaurants, and art galleries. It's bursting with street life and kaleidoscopic walls of colors and shapes.

The art district's epicenter is the alley behind Denver Central Market, a renovated, 14,000-square-foot warehouse of eateries, bars, and cafés. Look for decorated paint cans hanging from the overhead wires (like sneakers), which signify different artists' turf. In 2018 alone, the Urban Arts Fund, founded as part of Denver's Public Art Program, commissioned more than 60 new murals. It really says something about Denverites that they care enough about their home to enact laws and allocate tax dollars to transform the cityscape into colorful canvases. These expressions of the city's soul protect about 500,000 square feet of walls from vandalism.

Address Arts District is bordered by I-25 to the West, 1-70 to the North, Park Avenue West and Broadway to the South, and Larimer Street to the East, Denver, CO 80205, www.rinoartdistrict.org | **Getting there** RTD Rail to 38th & Blake Streets (A Line) | **Hours** Unrestricted | **Tip** Every piece of handcrafted pottery at Fenway Clayworks is as functional and beautiful as it is unique (3047 Lawrence Street, www.fenwayclayworks.com).

99___ Sunken Gardens
Denver's best Frisbee lawn

Frisbee toys hadn't even been invented when designs for Sunken Gardens Park were being completed in 1911. As it turns out, this flat, wide and, yes, sunken lawn is perfect for hurling circular plastic discs great distances. There are better fields in the city for competitive Ultimate Frisbee matches (contact Colorado Core Ultimate for year round leagues), but Sunken Gardens is big enough and hemmed in enough for ideal two-person tossing. Dogs are welcome, too – but only on leash.

Built on the site of an old city landfill, the park is a great example of urban repurposing. Netherlands-born Saco Rienk de Boer (1883–1974) served as Denver's premier landscape architect for three decades and designed the park, now part of the mosaic of greenspaces managed by the Denver Park and Parkway System. DeBoer also designed nearby Hungarian Freedom Park, another pleasing, triangle-shape greenspace, and many other public spaces around the city. He's remembered for championing small, neighborhood "pocket parks" that humanize urban landscapes, and he had a hand in designing Red Rocks Amphitheater (see ch. 95) and the Denver Botanic Gardens (see ch. 107).

Sunken Gardens Park is family-friendly with a children's playground, covered shelter, and picnic tables. The path looping the park is .8 miles and attracts walkers and joggers. The park also neighbors West High School, and the students lounging in the park's "forested vale" are ubiquitous. Cross Speer Boulevard and walk the Cherry Creek Trail to 13th Street, and there's a distinctive, colorful mural by French artist, Da Cruz. If you've been to the Alliance Française (see ch. 7), you'll instantly recognize the artist's style from that building's mural.

Biking here may be the best way to enjoy this park. Cherry Creek Trail connects with the city's vast network of biking trails. Make sure to stuff a Frisbee in your backpack.

Address Speer Boulevard and 8th Avenue, Denver, CO 80204, +1 (303) 458-4788, www.www.uncovercolorado.com/activities/sunken-gardens-park | Getting there Bus 52 to Bannock Street & Speer Boulevard | Hours Daily dawn–dusk | Tip The Washington Park Lawn Bowling Club was established in 1924 and offers free lessons in this polite sport during the warmer months (S Downing Street & Louisiana Avenue, www.washingtonparklawnbowlingclub.com).

100_ The Temple

Legacy architecture brimming with creativity

Tucked between the hustle and bustle of Five Points (see ch. 19) and RiNo (see ch. 98), Curtis Park is a quiet warren of old brick buildings and stately trees. And at the corner of Curtis and 14th Streets, the giant gray Temple building both defines and defies the neighborhood vibe.

Originally built in 1882 and reconstructed after fire in the 1890s, it served as a Jewish temple, a printing press, a Christian church, and a private home. The entity that eventually became the United Way charitable organization was started here, and Nirvana and Black Flag have performed here. It's most recent iteration self-identifies as a "contemporary artist haven."

Prominent 19th-century architects Harry W. J. and Frank E. Edbrooke designed the Temple building. Originally from Chicago, the brothers learned the trade from their father, who helped rebuild after the 1871 Chicago Fire. The Temple is a mere afterthought compared to the Eldebrooke family's other buildings, iconic local landmarks, like the Brown Palace Hotel, Oxford Hotel, and the Tabor Grand Opera House. This space is immense and rambling, and the current owner, Adam Gordon, deliberately offers affordable rent for artists to thrive. This is also the home of the Denver Zine Library, which recently expanded to the Denver Public Library branch at RiNo Art Park. This collection of 20,000-plus underground magazines showcases the beauty and innovation of self-published work, much of it presaging today's social media self-expression. The founders also host workshops and a zine festival.

The Temple is also home to Heirloom Catering, a proudly local, woman-owned champion of culinary arts, sustainable sourcing, and food-access equality. And on the other end of the spectrum, the building's anchor tenants, ShowLabs are wizards of digital content production. What is a city without art in all its mediums?

Address 2400 Curtis Street, Denver, CO 80205, www.thetempleartsdenver.org | Getting there Bus 44, 48 to Broadway & Arapahoe Street | Hours See website for events and open studio times | Tip The Armory was built in 1889 and was once home to the Colorado Militia. A former boxing gym where Sonny Liston trained and Jack Dempsey fought, it's now a concert venue, performance space, and recording studio (2565 Curtis Street, www.thearmorydenver.com).

101_ Tiny Town
Where it's ok to be a kid

Colorado is rich with historic narrow-gauge, steam-powered railroads that served mining towns. The Durango & Silverton and the Cumbres & Toltec (between Chama, New Mexico, and Antonito, Colorado) lines are perennial favorites. But in Morrison there's an even narrower variant. Pulled by an actual miniature steam locomotive, this little train chugs a 5/8-mile loop on tracks only 15 inches wide that look like toothpicks. It pulls open cars with benches for two people, and competition for the children-only caboose is fierce.

Originally opened in 1921, Tiny Town is a miniature village containing more than 100 1/6th-scale buildings and looped by the miniature railroad. It's the kind of place you'd imagine Pee-wee Herman as mayor and Barney the Dinosaur as train conductor. Silly and shamelessly fun, it's a children's paradise. If you haven't been back since you were a kid, now's the time.

Some of the buildings are historic scale replicas, like Denver's old County Jail from 1891. Some are modeled after pop culture, like the *Addams Family* mansion and the building in Grant Wood's *American Gothic* painting. Most of the buildings are just smaller versions of a real Western town. There's a gas station, a car dealership, a market, a barbershop, a radio station, and more. Many are fitted with authentic furniture and dolls. There's even Soapy Smith's Saloon (see ch. 22).

Tiny Town is the only place in Colorado where the gunslinger's maxim actually works: "This town ain't big enough for the two of us." Thankfully, the layout is spacious, immense evergreens offer pleasant shade over well-paced benches, and there's a playground for children to work out their excitement. The $3 railroad trip takes nine minutes and passes hillsides dotted with fun distractions, like mischievous trolls and the white-dotted mushrooms of fairy tales. Then head off for lunch in charming Evergreen.

Address 6249 S Turkey Creek Road, Morrison, CO 80465, +1 (303) 697-6829, www.tinytownrailroad.com | Getting there By car, take Highway 285 to S Turkey Creek Road | Hours Daily Mon–Fri 10am–4pm, Sat & Sun 10am–5pm (Memorial Day–Labor Day) | Tip The Colorado Railroad Museum showcases the real deal. These immense locomotives helped shape commerce and immigration to the state (17155 W 44th Avenue, Golden, www.coloradorailroadmuseum.org).

102 Titans of 17th Street

Walk down the Wall Street of the Rockies

A walk through the shaded canyons of these buildings is a visceral reminder that real money built this town. Businessmen are wont to puff up their chests to stir investor confidence, and financial districts across the western United States, in cities like San Francisco, Los Angeles, and Fort Worth, promoted themselves as Wall Street of the West. Denver real estate developers also used this term for Denver's 17th Street in the late 1900s then went one step further, designating these blocks "Wall Street of the Rockies."

To understand Denver is to understand the impact of mining, railroads, and oil and gas development on the regional economy. The first major commercial buildings representing these industries went up in the late 19th century, including the Denver Mint (see ch. 38). Adjacent to the State Capitol, 17th Street was the epicenter of finance for the Mountain West. The nine-story Equitable Building (730 17th Street) was completed in 1892 as Denver's first high-rise at 143 feet. The Boston Building (828 17th Street) and the Ideal Building (821 17th Street) are the other notable 19th-century, neoclassical, stone cathedrals to the god of money. And when the Colorado National Bank (918 17th Street) – now a luxury hotel – was completed in 1911, with its fantastic Native American murals by Allen Tupper True, a 17th Street address afforded its own legacy.

Today, Denver's snaggletooth skyline is reassuringly familiar, if not internationally distinctive. Seventeenth Street boasts Colorado's tallest building, the 56-story, 717-foot Republic Plaza (370 17th Street), but Wells Fargo's "Cash Register" building (1700 Lincoln Street) is the most recognizable. And in a telltale sign of the times, the shimmering glass Optiv Tower (1286 17th Street), which reflects the sky's mood and is Denver's most attractive skyscraper, is owned by a cybersecurity company.

Address 17th Street between Larimer Street & Broadway, Denver, CO 80202 | Getting there Bus 8, 48 to Curtis & 16th Street Mall; RTD Rail to 16th & California Streets (D, H, L Lines) | Hours Unrestricted | Tip The Pullman Guest Rooms on the second floor of Union Station's Crawford Hotel draw Art Deco design inspiration from the Pullman sleeper train cars (1701 Wynkoop Street, www.thecrawfordhotel.com).

103__ Tracks

The dance party never stops

This LGBTQ+ friendly nightclub throws down hard. Wear comfortable shoes (or red leather platform boots) because you're going to dance into the late night hours. Pride passions run high in Denver, and Tracks caters to this community with themed nights, drag queen performances, and guest DJs. There are multiple rooms with different vibes if you want to get lost in the music. The atmosphere can also be sexually charged, so be prepared for some flaunting. It's ok to be beautiful.

Denver's LGBTQ+ community is well represented in bars and businesses (and families) in the city, of course, but Tracks is deliberately insular. All are welcome, but the numbers skew heavily out. The tribe also parties at Trade, Gladys, Pride & Swagger, and Charlie's. In case you're wondering, Dream Canyon west of Boulder is known for gay cruising. Babes Around Denver (BAD) is a group of women who host the lesbian community at Tracks on the first Friday of every month for two-stepping and line dancing earlier in the evening, and they'll start playing more kinds of dance music later on. BAD's First Fridays are "the largest and longest running monthly women's party in the US," according to their website (www.babesaroundenver.com).

Today's culture has finally learned to recognize gender fluidity, and safe public places are important for experimenting with identity. The Center on Colfax (1301 E Colfax, lgbtqcolorado.org) is an excellent resource for this community. In the harsh light of day, the center offers a critically important range of services and programs for the entire rainbow.

It's fun to be in public with zero pretense (or, perhaps, maximum pretense!), and dancing at Tracks can be liberating. Nina Flowers, winner of *RuPaul's Drag Race*, has performed here, and there's an element of the outrageous. Sexual preferences span the spectrum, so let your freak flag fly at Tracks.

Address 3500 Walnut Street, Denver, CO 80205, +1 (303) 863-7326, www.tracksdenver.com, tracksinfo@tracksdenver.com | Getting there Bus 44 to Larimer & Downing Streets | Hours Wed–Sat 8pm–2am | Tip In a cool, historic building in the heart of downtown, the Triangle Bar is a stronghold of LGBTQ+ social life (2036 N Broadway, www.thetriangledenver.com).

104_ Turkey Creek Bridge

The murder of Adolf Coors III

On this unassuming road in the pretty foothills west of Denver, Adolf Coors III was murdered on February 9, 1960, in a kidnapping gone sideways. Coors was president and CEO of Coors Brewing Company and on top of the world at just 45 years old. He had attended Cornell University and even had a short career as a semi-professional baseball player before joining the family business. Coors was an avid sportsman and married with four young children, but fabulous wealth made him a target. Some say his aggrieved ghost still haunts the area.

Coors Brewing Company was founded in Golden on the banks of Clear Creek. A stone's throw from Turkey Creek Bridge in Morrison, Golden is synonymous with Coors Brewing Company. Coors liked to drive his International Harvester Travelall to see the beautiful red sandstone. When his station wagon was discovered with bloodstains, broken glasses, and his hat, local police shifted into high gear. The next day Coors' wife received a ransom note for $500,000, and the ensuing manhunt was nationwide, the largest since the deadly kidnapping of Charles Lindbergh's baby.

Seven months later, parts of Coors' body were discovered in the wilderness near Pikes Peak, along with his engraved pen knife and shirt. A tip then led investigators to an abandoned vehicle belonging to Joe Corbett, a former Colorado resident and convicted killer who'd escaped federal prison. A distinctive sediment from the Morrison area was discovered on the undercarriage of Corbett's car, and analysis of his typewriter proved it had produced the ransom note. The case against Corbett was built entirely on forensic evidence and earned the emerging science newfound credibility. The Coors murder had no eyewitnesses, but Corbett was convicted of first-degree murder and spent 29 years in jail. He maintained his innocence until the bitter end, committing suicide at age 80.

Address S Turkey Creek Road, Morrison, CO 80465 | **Getting there** By car, US Highway 285 to S Turkey Creek Road | **Hours** Unrestricted | **Tip** In 1941, vagrant Theodore Coneys murdered the owner of this Highlands home and then lived like a spider in the attic for 10 months before being caught, earning the nickname, "Denver Spiderman" (3335 West Moncrieff Place).

105_ Twist & Shout
Where vinyl gathers no dust

Does your copy of *Shatner Claus* have a fatal scratch on "Little Drummer Boy"? Well, fans of *Star Trek's* William Shatner need look no further for his Christmas album. Founded in 1988, Twist & Shout Records never abandoned vinyl and no record is too random for the music aficionados who work here. Rummage the 11,000 square feet, and you'll find rare, out-of-print, and imported vinyl from every artist and genre under the sun. In addition to buying and selling vinyl, there's an entire room of CDs, DVDs, and Blu-ray.

Owners Paul and Jill Epstein have consistently nurtured local and traveling artists by selling, trading, and promoting wide genres of music and shows, including hosting live shows in the store. The walls are covered in album art and historic memorabilia, like a remnant of the original sign for the Rainbow Ballroom, a hopping local dance hall from 1933 – 1961, where touring big bands were guaranteed to play – everyone from Louis Armstrong and Duke Ellington to Lawrence Welk and Chuck Berry.

The meticulous album curation on display here caters to customers looking for their favorite bands, of course, but the shop's lifeblood is collectors. Building up a vinyl collection is a point of pride to serious music lovers, and Twist & Shout Records is a mandatory stop on the picking circuit. (Let's not forget that venerable record player company Victrola is based in Denver, too.)

Twist & Shout's $6 Grab Bags are a particular pleasure. Unlabeled and wrapped in brown paper, these 10-record collections are randomly selected and filled with surprises. As one staffer quipped, "They're full of good stuff in bad shape, and bad stuff in good shape." Twist & Shout shares the building with the Sie FilmCenter, a cinematheque and event space that shows arthouse movies and international films. And you're walking distance to The Fillmore, Bluebird, and Ogden live music venues.

Address 2508 E Colfax Avenue, Denver, CO 80206, +1 (303) 722-1943,
www.twistandshout.com | Getting there Bus 15 to Colfax Avenue & Detroit Street |
Hours Mon–Sat 10am–7pm, Sun 10am–6pm | Tip Wax Trax Records is smaller
and grungier but great for picking and offers personalized customer service
(638 E 13th Avenue, www.waxtraxrecords.com).

106 Union Station Farm Market

Small-town feel in the big city

If Union Station is "Denver's Living Room," then the Union Station Farmers Market is our social hour. This is where locals wander, shop, and chat. This explosion of colors and smells is a bright counterpoint to the surrounding hubbub of concrete and steel. Held next to a massive fountain and whimsical public sculptures, this farmers market is one of many across the Front Range, which remains staunchly agricultural despite the population boom. The Union Station Farmers Market is a key outgrowth of Union Station's $54 million Beaux Arts revitalization completed in 2012.

Held on Saturdays from spring through the fall, this farmers market humanizes Denver with the wholesome goodness. Farmers markets are unabashedly positive and friendly, and browsing and shopping at this one market is a dreamy pleasure. Welcoming vendors sell a cornucopia of fresh, organic, local produce, meats, and baked goods and offer delectable sample bites. There's always live music and community tables for noshing and gossiping. This small-town feeling in the big city is irreplaceable. Come and pet peoples' dogs, and enjoy the morning.

There's been a train hub in LoDo since 1881, thanks to Colorado's central location at the crossroads of the nation. Colorado connected to the transcontinental railroad via Cheyenne, Wyoming in 1870. Commerce exploded as a result, and new ideas, people, and goods came with rail traffic, earning Colorado statehood. By 1880 the Centennial State had 1,500 miles of rails.

Inside Union Station, the couches and ample public seating offer a welcoming, intimate feel. Natural light pours in from immense windows and reflects off pendulous chandeliers 65 feet up. Heck, if you can't tear yourself away, book a night in the station's lovely Crawford Hotel.

Address 1701 Wynkoop Street, Denver, CO 80202, www.bcfm.org/home-page/
denver-union-station, community@bcfm.org | Getting there RTD Rail to Union
Station (A, B, E, G, N, W Lines) | Hours Sat 9am–1pm (May–Oct) | Tip Denver
Bread Company, founded by Gregory Bortz in 1994, is a neighborhood boulangerie
serving fresh-baked artisan breads of world-class quality (3200 Irving Street,
www.thedenverbreadcompany.com).

107__ Urban Nature Bathing
Bamboo forest bliss

The Japanese practice of forest bathing (*shinrin-yoku*) soothes and calms. You're meant to immerse yourself in natural settings and allow nature to wash over your senses. Do just that in the diffuse light and vibrant greens of June's Plant Asia garden at the Denver Botanic Gardens. Find the path under the towering forest of bamboo and prepare to relax.

There are five outdoor gardens like this here, each designed to bathe frazzled modern psyches in the diverse bio-regions of planet Earth. Verdant lawns and towering trees, cactus and succulents, gurgling water features and tea houses call visitors to wander for hours. Exhibits transition abruptly from the serenity of the bonsai gardens to the severity of alpine environments to flower-dense ornamental gardens. The 24 acres are jam-packed, so pace yourself.

The *Amorphophallus titanum* from Sumatra, Indonesia, aka the Corpse Flower, has its own special area, too. It smells like, you guessed it, a decomposing body and requires special care and sequestration. These giant flowers can grow to 10 feet tall, radiating a pungent scent when blooming that attracts flesh-eating insects to spread pollen. This is not the place to forest bathe, but it is a strange sensation to see the plant's center, which resembles a phallus the size of an adult human.

The architectural boldness of the buildings hold their own, as well. The signature Boettcher Memorial Tropical Conservatory is a steamy pyramid of glass. An enveloping atrium that traps musty heat and sweet smells, it contains plants from lowland tropical rainforests. The jumble of shapes, colors, and odors is intoxicating (*shinrin-yoku!*). This atrium alone contains 3,177 taxa, representing more than 2,375 plant species from 706 genera and 124 families. Well-represented, and satisfyingly morbid, are the insect-eating *Dionaea muscipula* (Venus fly trap) and *Nepenthes* (pitcher plants).

Address 1007 York Street, Denver, CO 80206, +1 (720) 865-3500, www.botanicgardens.org |
Getting there Bus 24 to Josephine Street & 9th Avenue | Hours Daily 9am–4pm | Tip
Neighboring Cheesman Park is the site of a 19th-century cemetery, once known as the Old
Boneyard, where unclaimed bodies were dumped in unmarked graves. The 80 gorgeous acres
and pavilion here are said to be haunted after city workers disturbed the dead.

108__ VFW Post #1
The original refuge

Since its founding in Denver in 1899, the Veterans of Foreign Wars (VFW) organization was founded in 1899 here at VFW1, the first and oldest post. The VFW has grown to more than 6,000 posts worldwide and 1.6 million members. It's no longer a rite of passage for young Americans to be drafted or enlist into the Armed Forces. Declining, aging, and largely male membership in the 1990s forced VFW Post 1 to reinvent itself or risk losing its charter.

The group's newly renovated building in the Santa Fe Art District is surrounded by art galleries and welcomes the general public. The VFW Post 1 displays artwork by veterans and hosts frequent cultural activities, including painting classes and yoga workshops. Perhaps most importantly, alcohol is no longer central to the experience here, save for the occasional whiskey tasting. This is a healing place for the community and for veterans, many of whom suffer from post-traumatic stress disorder (PTSD) and need support. Today's post membership is younger and counts more women veterans.

Colorado's General Irving Hale (1861–1930) co-founded the VFW after serving in the Spanish-American War and the Philippine-American War, where he earned a Silver Star. Camp Hale, the Colorado training ground for the 10th Mountain Division, was named after him in 1942. These distinctions forever tie Colorado to the American ski industry because Camp Hale-trained winter troops returned home from World War II and founded the country's first ski resorts, including Vail. These troops also founded the National Ski Patrol, headquartered in Colorado, of course.

Coloradans can also take pride in the VFW for lobbying after World War I, along with the American Legion (which is open to all veterans, not just those who fought in foreign wars), to pressure the federal government to allocate dollars for veteran healthcare and education.

Address 841 Santa Fe Drive, Denver, CO 80204, +1 (720) 515-8391, www.vfwpost1.org, admin@vfwpost1.org | **Getting there** Bus 1 to Santa Fe Drive & W 8th Avenue | **Hours** See website for event schedule | **Tip** The Colorado Veterans Monument, or Veterans Obelisk, on the west side of the Colorado State Capitol is a stalwart 30-foot obelisk. The red sandstone was mined in Lyons, and the inlaid bronze plaques honor the five branches of the Armed Forces (1449 Lincoln Street).

109 Western Daughters Butcher Shoppe

Old-world artistry with big knives

Western Daughters "heirloom" Butcher Shoppe quarters the entire animal, thus eliminating the supply chain. The beef and pork sold here is only sourced locally, grass-fed, and pasture-raised. Purchased directly from ranchers, the animals sold here are humanely raised and slaughtered with transparency. Co-owner Kate Kavanaugh aims to "revive the West one pasture at a time," by only sourcing animals within a 150-mile radius of Denver. She also offers CSA shares, pay-in-advance Community Supported Agriculture, that allows investment in restorative agriculture.

Kavanaugh's great grandmother was an Irish immigrant with five daughters, a widow who set out for Colorado in a covered wagon. She deliberately builds on the area's ranching legacy. Larry McMurtry's Pulitzer prize-winning novel *Lonesome Dove* is loosely based on Charles Goodnight and Oliver Loving, the Texas cattlemen who pioneered the Goodnight-Loving cattle trail in 1866. The herds would pass through Denver on the way to Cheyenne, Wyoming. After the Civil War, soldiers returned to Texas and found that neglected free-range cattle had multiplied vigorously. With limited options to monetize the abundance locally, cattlemen organized cattle drives north to railheads in Kansas. This beef bonanza only lasted about 20 years, but it spawned the immortal myth of the American Cowboy. Colorado ranchers made use of abundant land throughout northeastern Colorado, and the local beef industry was born.

Western Daughters Butcher Shoppe is small and cozy. Fresh cuts of prime meats glisten, and the staff is informative and friendly. The real value, however, is becoming a member of the Meat Club CSA. At an average cost of $10.75 per pound of fresh meat, you can grill ribeye steaks every week.

Address 3326 Tejon Street, Denver, CO 80211, +1 (303) 477-6328, www.westerndaughters.com | Getting there Bus 44 to Tejon Street & W 34th Avenue | Hours Daily 10am–7pm | Tip Tony's Meats & Market opened in 1978. This excellent, community-centric butcher also has fresh-baked goods, local produce, and fine cheeses (three locations in the Denver Metro Area, www.tonysmarket.com).

110 Wild Animal Sanctuary

Where exotic animals retire

The 800-acre facility in the grasslands northeast of Denver is hard to describe. It's not a zoo, but exotic captive animals do live here. It's not a ranch, but many of the animals roam gigantic outdoor enclosures. It is not an exploitative breeding ground, and about 100 large carnivores from the horrific (and hypnotically entertaining) *Tiger King* Netflix series have been rehomed here. Private ownership of top predators is often a slow motion train wreck, but the animals who find their way here will never be abused or neglected again. This is forever-home heaven.

The nonprofit Wild Animal Sanctuary is a "federally licensed zoological facility" that opened in 1980. No animals are bred or sold here. The endangered carnivores who retire here were mostly confiscated from the illegal pet trade or from ignorant owners. The animals live out their days here, everything from coatimundi and foxes to alpaca and camels to lions and tigers. There are wading pools and temperature-controlled dens. There's even a 1,900-pound Kodiak bear, and all the bears get to hibernate underground.

Seeing a bobcat, lynx, or mountain lion is exciting, but spend any time in the Rockies, and you will see these species in the wild. Nothing, however, compares to looking an apex predator in the eye. To be sized up by the absolute power of a large, man-eating carnivore is almost a mystical experience. You can see it all here along 1.5 miles of elevated walkways.

Caring for the animals requires a small army of 53 full-time staff and more than 150 regular volunteers to feed the animals 85,000 pounds of fresh food per week. A big cat can live for more than 20 years, so that's a lot of cat litter – and money. The large animals can cost $8,000 a year in feed, housing, and veterinary care. You'll soon be evangelizing to eliminate the US illegal pet trade and educating your friends.

Address 2999 CO Road 53, Keenesburg, CO 80643, www.wildanimalsanctuary.org |
Getting there By car, take I-76 E to Exit 31, go east at Exit 31 to CO-52, turn right on
CO Road 53 | Hours Daily 9am–dusk | Tip Just up the road, Pawnee National Grassland
is a 193,000-acre oasis of pristine prairie. Buffalo did roam here, but today it's primarily a
birding destination (115 N 2nd Avenue, Ault, www.uncovercolorado.com/national-lands/
pawnee-national-grassland).

111_ The Wizard's Chest

Middle Earth come to life

First opened in 1983, the Wizard's Chest toy store was designed to look like something from a J. R. R. Tolkien book. The magical weirdness of the place is joyfully extravagant. There are strange metal minarets on the building's roof, making it look like a steampunk castle. And the entrance is decked out with a suit of armor and a giant, metal wizard. It's axiomatic that any 16,000 square-foot building that's painted purple is worth visiting.

Yes, there are mountains of toys here, including oddities like heavy metal swords, and an especially impressive puzzle selection. One favorite area, though, is the wig section, where you can choose from wigs of every color, length, and style. A chatty salesperson may tell you that Denver's drag queens come here to shop for quality and durability. "When you're on stage every night dancing and sweating, you want a wig that holds up to abuse and regular washing," he explained. They're fun for kids playing dress-up too.

There's also an impressive section devoted to magic. Magicians never reveal their tricks, but this is where they come to learn them. All the paraphernalia and tools of the trade include detailed instructions. The sales staff here at the "professional magic counter" is conspiratorially adamant that practice is the key to pulling off convincing illusions.

As fun as it is to play with all the toys, wigs, and swords, the store's murals, decorations, and wall art are perhaps more impressive. There's a giant elephant hanging from the ceiling and huge murals of dancing animals. The old posters, sculls, maps, and strange devices give the place a feeling of the occult. Kids old and young can easily spend some time here. The costume section alone can swallow you up, and the wheel-chair accessible ramp to the lower floor is transformed into a maze. There's also a game room for special events and playing the fantasy card game Magic.

Address 451 Broadway, Denver, CO 80203, +1 (303) 321-4304, www.wizardschest.com |
Getting there Bus 0 to Broadway & 5th Avenue | **Hours** Mon–Fri 11am–7pm, Sat &
Sun 10am–7pm | **Tip** Right next door, Axe Whooping offers indoor axe throwing and
a "rage room," where you break stuff, basically. There are seven axe-throwing businesses
in Denver at last count. Some even serve alcohol, which seems crazy (437 Broadway,
www.axewhooping.com).

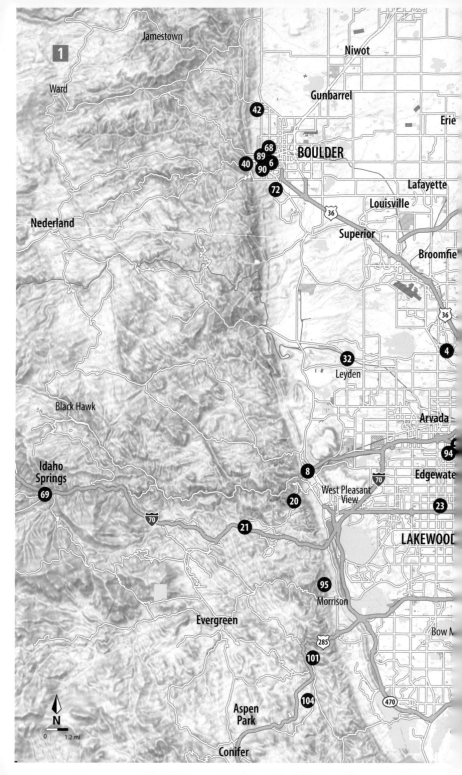

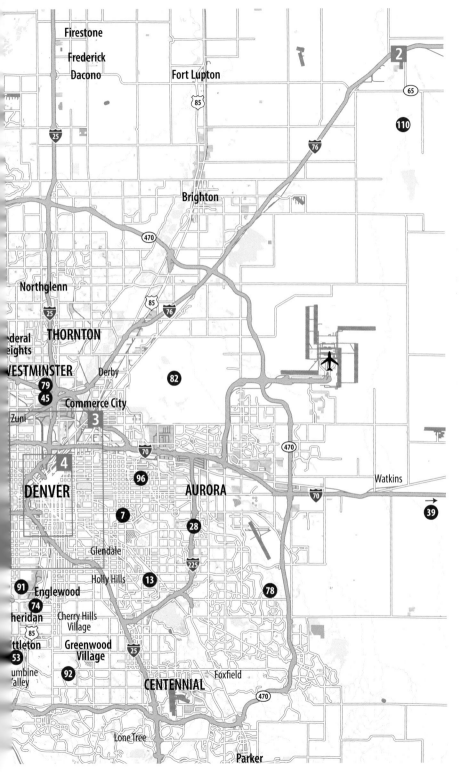

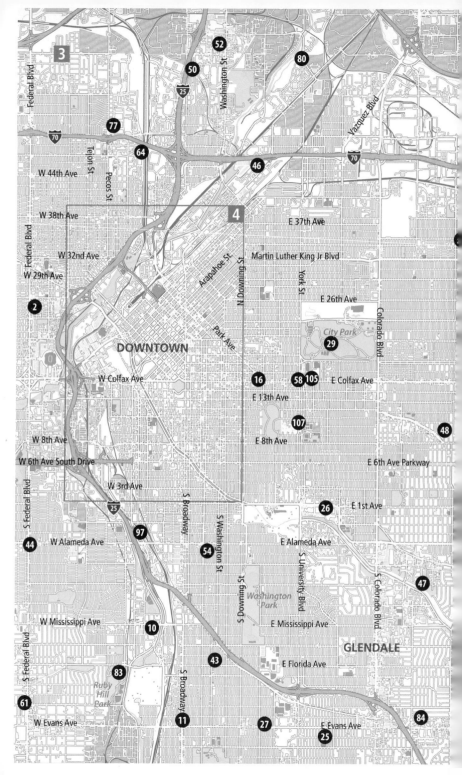

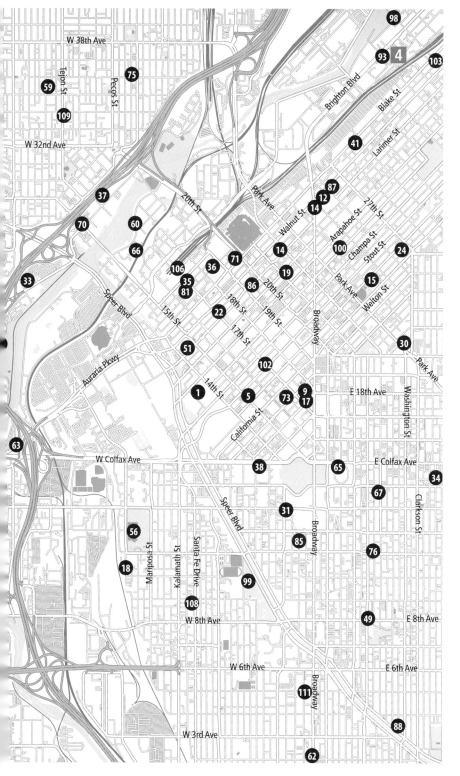

Amy Bizzarri, Susie Inverso
111 Places in Chicago
That You Must Not Miss
ISBN 978-3-7408-1030-6

Amy Bizzarri, Susie Inverso
111 Places for Kids in Chicago
That You Must Not Miss
ISBN 978-3-7408-0599-9

Elizabeth Foy Larsen
111 Places in the Twin Cities
That You Must Not Miss
ISBN 978-3-7408-1347-5

Dana DuTerroil, Joni Fincham,
Daniel Jackson
111 Places in Houston
That You Must Not Miss
ISBN 978-3-7408-0896-9

Kelsey Roslin, Nick Yeager,
Jesse Pitzler
111 Places in Austin
That You Must Not Miss
ISBN 978-3-7408-0748-1

Travis Swann Taylor
111 Places in Atlanta
That You Must Not Miss
ISBN 978-3-7408-0747-4

Katrina Nattress, Jason Quigley
111 Places in Portland
That You Must Not Miss
ISBN 978-3-7408-0750-4

Harriet Baskas
111 Places in Seattle
That You Must Not Miss
ISBN 978-3-7408-1219-5

Floriana Petersen, Steve Werney
111 Places in San Francisco
That You Must Not Miss
ISBN 978-3-95451-609-4

Laurel Moglen, Julia Posey,
Lyudmila Zotova
**111 Places in Los Angeles
That You Must Not Miss**
ISBN 978-3-7408-0906-5

Jo-Anne Elikann
**111 Places in New York
That You Must Not Miss**
ISBN 978-3-95451-052-8

Evan Levy, Rachel Mazor,
Joost Heijmenberg
**111 Places for Kids in New York
That You Must Not Miss**
ISBN 978-3-7408-1218-8

Kim Windyka, Heather Kapplow,
Alyssa Wood
**111 Places in Boston
That You Must Not Miss**
ISBN 978-3-7408-1558-5

Andréa Seiger, John Dean
**111 Places in Washington
That You Must Not Miss**
ISBN 978-3-7408-1560-8

Allison Robicelli, John Dean
**111 Places in Baltimore
That You Must Not Miss**
ISBN 978-3-7408-0158-8

Michelle Madden, Janet McMillan
**111 Places in Milwaukee
That You Must Not Miss**
ISBN 978-3-7408-0491-6

Sandra Gurvis, Mitch Geiser
**111 Places in Columbus
That You Must Not Miss**
ISBN 978-3-7408-0600-2

Cristyle Egitto, Jakob Takos
**111 Places in Palm Beach
That You Must Not Miss**
ISBN 978-3-7408-1452-6

Photo Credits:

All photos by Susie Inverso, except:

Buell Public Media Center (ch. 19): courtesy of Rocky Mountain Public Media

Lakeside Amusement Park (ch. 57): courtesy of Lakeside Park Company

NOAA Boulder (ch. 72): Will von Dauster, courtesy of NOAA

Tracks (ch. 103): Brian Degenfelder, courtesy of Tracks Nightclub

Art Credits:

Cold War Horse (ch. 32): Jeff Gipe

Fairy Doors (ch. 43): Michelle Brown

Spirit of the West (ch. 95): Sue DeCicco Smith

Tiny Workers (ch 98): Juane

Untitled (ch. 100): Thomas "Detour" Evans

My journalism career would never have launched as it did without the initial mentorship of Nancy Zimmerman. Jon Dorn made this book contract possible thanks to his stalwart support. Karen Seiger (my editor at Emons) brilliantly improved the manuscript. The encouragement of my father Philip means more to my adult self than I care to admit. My children R. and G. make life worth living. Jane, you are the journey and the destination – our love powers my world. My brothers, well, they smell funny.
Philip D. Armour

I'd like to express my deepest thanks to my husband, Justin, who first brought me to visit Colorado on our honeymoon, and then agreed – after my compelling slide presentation – that we should live here. He accompanied me on many of these treks as navigator, assistant, and model. We had a blast exploring our new city for this book! I'd also like to thank Karen Seiger for this third assignment in the *111 Places* series. It has been an honor to have photographed two books for my home-town of Chicago and now one for my new town of Denver for Emons.
Susie Inverso

Philip D. Armour is a freelance journalist, editor, and author based in Colorado's Front Range. Published everywhere from *The New York Times* to *Outside*, he's equally comfortable skinning up 14ers and navigating Denver's backstreets. Philip has been enamored with "Paris on the Platte" since first visiting in 1992. If you're ever at Brother's Bar, please pay his tab.

Susie Inverso has now photographed three books in the *111 Places* series. After spending her entire life in Chicago, she and her husband relocated to Denver so they could enjoy the beauty of the mountains! When not hiking, biking, or skiing, Susie runs Crimson Cat Studios where she helps pet-parents celebrate, honor, and tell the saga of their non-human family members through photography. She and her husband are enjoying life in Lakewood with their two cats and box turtle.